HARVEST THE LIGHT
A YOUNG MAN'S REACTIONS

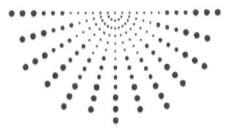

TOM RUBENS

Copyright © 2020 by Tom Rubens

All rights reserved.

The right of Tom Rubens to be identified as author of this work has been asserted by him in accordance with section 77 and 78 of the Copyright, Designs and Patents Act 1988.

All rights reserved. No part of this publication may be reproduced, stored in a retrieval system, or transmitted in any form or by any means, electronic, mechanical, photocopying, recording, or otherwise, without the prior permission of the publishers.

Any person who commits any unauthorised act in relation to this publication may be liable to criminal prosecution and civil claims for damages.

Cover Design and typography by Louise Taylor

Happy London Press : Independent Publishing for new authors enabling them to express there talents.

ISBN: 978-1-912951-34-5 Paperback

ISBN: 978-1-912951-35-2 Hardback

ISBN: 978-1-912951-36-9 Ebook

In memory of W. Somerset Maugham, whose outstanding novel Of Human Bondage (1915) was in the back of my mind while I was writing this book.

Dedication to my best friend Vladimir Dirsh

 Tom Rubens has been a teacher of English in further and higher education for most of his working life. In addition to the present book, he has published eight books on Philosophy, and a selection of poems. He is active politically, and in local community affairs.

HARVEST THE LIGHT

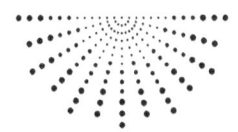

CHAPTER ONE

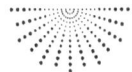

REFLECTING ON HIS RESOLUTENESS TO CONTINUE SEEING PINA, DESPITE her mother's opposition, Richard found himself seething with thoughts, about a range of things. He valued Pina's courage in going against her mother, the more so because this was a social context very different from the one he had been used to in England, and which he knew was similar in other countries where traditional parental authority had waned. He was now seeing Pina, with her gumption and intelligence, as a kind of representative of a new generation of young people in hitherto tradition-bound societies: a new generation that was seeking to break free of old and stifling conventions.

At the same time, he was acutely aware that his respect and hope for her filled a space which was unaccompanied by one consisting of feelings of sexual love. So, the future he wished for her was one he could not share with her. That future would unfold in a different place from the place he would, before much longer, be in.

But, in the meantime, he was determined to make the most of the unquestionable rapport he shared with her: something which, he felt, was as important as anything else, and which was worth protecting from anyone or any thing threatening its continuance.

The following Sunday, when he got off the bus at the station, he had no difficulty in remembering the way to Pina's house. He pressed the doorbell. The door opened, and Pina stood with smiling, rounded face, her head turning slightly and her eyes seeming to drink from his. Her hair was done up at the back with a small ribbon.

"You are here, Richard."

He smiled, and she asked him to come in while she got her things. The living room was empty. Through the half-open kitchen door, he saw Mrs Barrios, her back to him, standing washing dishes at the sink. She did not look round.

"Shall we go, Richard?"

His eyes went to Pina. Her coat was on her arm. "Yes," he replied, wondering where her father was.

Outside, she closed the door behind her, with, "Last night it was orr-eeble," hand upturned and fingers outspread.

"What happened?"

"I told my mother you were coming this morning and there was a very big argument. In the end, she said I could do just what I wanted. She said she was no more interested."

"And your father?"

"He did not say anything. And this morning, he went out early, perhaps because he was afraid of being friendly toward you in front of her." She exhaled, but then a gradual smile spread across her lips. "Anyway, now I can be with you as much as I want."

He said nothing, but smiled in return. They walked toward the station and he bought two tickets for the trip to Cintra.

They waited for the train on the platform, which was, once more, crowded with families. Pina glanced at him the way she had before. Again, he smiled, but said nothing.

The train shunted slowly in, and its passengers got out.

The crowds starting moving forward, and Pina's hand tightened in his. "We can go to the first carriage,"

They started walking, her leading, him still smiling. But then she stopped, her eyes fixed on a point to his left.

He looked across and saw a policeman in the grey-blue uniform which had become familiar to him. Beside the policeman was another man wearing a suit.

"Ah," she said. "The one in the suit may be from the P.I.D.E."

"The security police?"

"Yes, but I do not know why they should be here. Perhaps they have been given information about someone coming to this station."

They continued to the carriage door, and he turned the handle to open it. Inside, they chose seats in the corner.

Then they looked out of the window and saw that the two men were still standing in the same position. The train jolted and began moving.

Returning to their seats, they held hands again. She said, "This is a very bad country."

"Because of the P.I.D.E.?"

"Yes, but really because of the government. The P.I.D.E. is just an instrument of the government."

She stopped, and glanced around the carriage: he felt he knew the reason. The only other occupants were two families, busily talking amongst themselves. There was nobody sitting alone and looking in their direction. Her eyes went back to his: "You always have to be careful," her voice slightly lower than before, as if by reflex. "They could have been here."

"I see what you mean."

"The government needs the P.I.D.E. because it is a fascist government. They do not permit elections, and they are fighting wars in Africa – in Angola and Mozambique."

"How long have these wars being going on?"

"Nearly ten years. The government is fighting to hold the last parts of its empire."

"And the P.I.D.E. keeps check on everything going on in this country?"

"Yes. They are everywhere." She went on to tell him about the P.I.D.E. agents who rode the trams, the metro, the railway trains, and even posed as street-hawkers to catch the conversation of passers-by. They also mingled in cafe crowds. When they infiltrated university student groups, student protesters were arrested and imprisoned without trial.

In addition, workers could not form unions. Portugal had had no unions for forty years, not since the rise to power of the dictator Salazar, who had just died and been replaced by someone equally dictatorial – Caetano.

Suddenly she stopped, went wide-eyed and brought her fingertips to her lips. "Ah, I know I am rushing from one thing to another. But I am always like this. Because there are so many things. So mány," with a slight waist-shoulder turn. "Now, I will tell you just one."

Going slower now, she described something that had happened while she was at university. A protest group had started an underground newspaper; it was circulated to all colleges in Lisbon and to the university of Coimbra. She was one of the subscribers. All the people involved knew they were risking imprisonment but continued with the paper for nearly nine months.

Eventually the police found out about it, though they were not given any names. They got ready to raid the printing office. The office staff were warned in advance and got away just in time, but they forgot to take the subscribers' list with them.

One morning, she received a letter ordering her to come to police headquarters. On arrival, she saw she was one of thirty students who had been called in for questioning. They were interrogated separately, each for about 20 minutes. The police wanted the names of the office staff and printers, and threatened an indefinite term of imprisonment for anyone withholding information. At that time, she added, there was a lot of protest activity, and the police were even harsher than usual in their threats.

"But," she said, "we told them nothing." Then, with a demure blink, a smile, and a turn of her head upwards, she put out her chin.

He had a sense of her parodying yet savouring a gesture of collective pride. He asked: "What did they do then?"

"They let us go."

"They didn't use violence?"

She shook her head, still with the smile. "I think they saw our determination." Then, "But also, perhaps, their prisons didn't have room for thirty persons more," the smile becoming a grin.

She had, he reflected, shown a kind of courage which he had never displayed, and for a moment he felt something he hadn't imagined he could feel toward her: a kind of envy. But the feeling passed, replaced by thoughts of her animated gestures, and of her desire for him, which could not be reciprocated. He asked: "Do you still see the people who were involved in this?"

"Yes, sometimes. Some of them still go to meetings at the university."

"Was the newspaper able to start again?"

"No. But after some time, the students made some organisations which the police permitted."

"Are they still operating?"

"Yes, but they cannot do much." She exhaled, her eyes turning to the windows. "It will be a long time before the students are really free, and before this country is free."

As the train pulled into Cintra station, Richard could see the town's surrounding hills: light-brown, with green copses, interspersed with small castles, some of which had coloured spires. He smiled at the extreme picturesqueness of the view, and reflected that this was all part of Portugal's past: a past which, no matter how complex, was very different from the complexities of the present.

Pina's head leaned toward his: "You see that castle on the left? The one with the orange-coloured walls?"

"Yes."

"That is where Lord Byron stayed."

"Oh, right."

Outside the station, there were a number of horse-drawn carriages waiting by the pavement.

"This is special to Cintra," said Pina. "It is – how do you say it – a tourist attraction."

"Well, shall we be tourists?"

"Ah, but the coaches are expensive."

"That's all right. Shall we go up to Byron's castle?"

She nodded with eagerness. In her gesture, he saw a reflection of her desire.

She gave instructions to the driver, and they made themselves comfortable in the wide, soft, black-leather seats. She held his hand in both of hers. The horse went into a trot, then slowed when the road grew steep. As they rose higher and higher, he felt a certain readiness to be open with her about his sexual position. He would, he resolved, soon make it clear. But meanwhile he accepted the fact of her desire because it was something positive. When the moment came to say what had to be said, he would not exactly be rejecting that positive, only indicating it must be re-directed. He did not want to undermine or reduce her desire, only to see it change course, while remaining fresh and full.

The carriage reached the castle gates. When Richard asked the driver the fare, he was pleasantly surprised that it wasn't as much as he'd expected.

Pina pointed to an inscription above the gate which gave details of Byron's stay. Inside the castle, they looked at various rooms. Byron's quarters were hung with richly embroidered draperies, and also had swords and pistols on the walls. At the sight of the latter, Richard smiled slightly, feeling distant from the uncomplicated kind of masculinity they suggested. Then they crossed the courtyard and went up a stone staircase to the ramparts. From there, Richard looked down at the thick-shadowed silence of the trees on the slopes below, then up and across, at the blueness of the land-line.

He felt Pina's palm on his ribs. It moved to the small of his back. Now, he realised, was the time for what had to be said. He turned from her, but more abruptly than he had intended – it was almost a wrenching movement.

"Where are you going?" she asked, but almost child-like, not hard-voiced. Yet despite the tone, he found the question oppressive. It put him in thought of being possessed without desiring, and he felt an alien sensation in his nostrils, like stale air in an enclosed space. He considered the harsh tension of being possessed, but then the thought passed; he instinctively felt that with her there would be no possessiveness, no harshness. He turned his eyes to hers, which showed pained confusion, though not anger. Quietly, she asked, "What is the matter?"

He replied. He spoke more simply than he had thought he would be able to: just a few words. The brevity only made it more important for him to add, "But I want to go on seeing you."

The brown of her eyes had less light now; it contained a trace of fatigue, and she said nothing.

"I couldn't pretend," he went on, "not about this."

Then he let the silence take its course. He would not oblige her to say anything it she did not want to. She leant against the rampart, and her eyes looked out into the distance. After a few minutes, they came back to his.

"I thought," she began, "that perhaps it was that. But I did not want to think so. I am glad you told me, and did not... use me." She breathed out.

In response to her words, he nodded.

"To say the truth," she continued, "I was surprised when you first showed interest in me. Someone like me, who is fat." Then, "Is there anyone who excites you in the way I do not?"

"No one," he replied, "whom I can talk to as I can to you."

"Thank you for saying that."

"It's simply the truth."

She took his hand in hers and held it gently; then said, "I would like to tell you about something that happened to me two years ago."

"Yes?"

"He was," she went on, "a student, in my class. I felt desire for him, though he felt nothing for me. I felt desire, but realised I could not talk with him. We shared nothing. Really we were strangers."

"I know what you mean. I know exactly."

"I am telling you this because I feel that sometimes desire… how can I say…?"

"Has its own driving force, independent of personality, and sometimes directly opposed to it?"

"Yes, just so. Like a force – like a force from outside you."

He nodded; her phrasing, though simpler, struck him as better than his. "From outside you," he repeated. Then: "But of course it isn't really," thinking once again about the processes of physical excitement, and how precisely they could be identified.

"No," she agreed. Her eyes lowered, and her thumb moved slightly over his knuckles. He wondered if this gesture indicated she too was thinking about these processes, specifically in relation to him.

She raised her eyes. "When I said before that I was surprised when you first showed an interest in me, I should also have said that I thought it would not be long before you lost interest in me."

"But I haven't," immediately.

"I can see. But many men would have. I know I am not the kind of girl who excites men."

These words made him think of Paul, then of Jennie. Almost automatically, he said, "Don't say that about yourself."

"But it was clear to me long ago, Richard. I could tell from men's eyes when they first saw me."

Feeling this had probably been the case, he could think of nothing to reply. He reflected on his own tendency, when seeing a woman for the first time, to consider whether he found her physically attractive.

"So," she echoed, "I know."

"Look," his mind returning to the sense of closeness with her, "I've said it doesn't matter."

"Yes," her eyes now softly on his. "Yes, you did."

"Now why," smiling, "don't we just think about other things?" Then. "Let's go and have some coffee."

She nodded, smiling slightly.

They sat at a cafe with a view of the sea in the distance. As they drank, their eyes passed undemandingly across each other's. He could detect no trace of resentment in her, and was not surprised at this.

He glanced into the distance to a point on the horizon where a strip of sea spanned a dip in the land. "See over there," pointing at arm's length. She looked. They both had to squint to see clearly. The sides of the dip were hill-slopes tinged pale blue. She said, "When it is very hot, the hills look a deeper blue."

"As in Van Gogh."

"Yes, or Cezanne. Or Lorraine."

Noting her knowledge of art, he turned to her. She was still looking out at the spot, using her hand as a shield from the sun. Her mind, it seemed, was now far removed from thoughts of her physical unattractiveness. He poured some more coffee into her cup from the pot the waiter had left.

They spent the rest of the afternoon looking at two other castles, sometimes with hands joined, sometimes not. The sun gradually lowered in the sky, and finally dropped behind the hill-line. Its after-light, diffusion of a flare that was now down out of sight, stood mellow orange between the dark hills and the faint blue that would soon fade to black.

He knew, and knew she did too, that they could not go very far into night together. Night was a region where, for him, needs would arise which she could not meet.

They boarded the train at the station; it was now half-empty; and he assumed that most of the people who had been with them on the journey out had gone back earlier. As the lights of farmhouses sped across the dark window of their carriage, they talked, not in a forced way, about the political situation. Then the train pulled into Lisbon. They walked along the platform, still on their subject, and out into the street.

"I'll see you home," he said.

"But it is only a short way."

"I'd like to," he insisted.

"All right."

When they reached the end of her street, he touched his lips to her forehead. She quickly touched hers to his cheek. He smiled: "Till tomorrow."

As he walked to the tram stop, the lights of the high part of the city were spread out before him, and he found himself thinking of bars and cafes where there would be physically exciting women. But the thought passed, replaced by considerations of the lesson preparation he would have to complete by the next morning.

CHAPTER TWO

RICHARD THOUGHT HE RECOGNISED THE HANDWRITING ON THE envelope that lay in his pigeon-hole in the school foyer. It was small lettering in blue fountain-pen ink. 'Paul,' he said to himself as he picked the envelope up.

Paul began the letter by asking him how he was finding Portugal, and how his teaching was going. Then he said that he had started his accountancy course, and that it was 'okay'. Richard paused at this adjective, which was somewhere between positive and negative, and recalled Paul's decision to opt for professional safety rather than adventure or risk-taking.

Paul then spoke about Freda, in a way reminiscent of what he had once said: that Richard was the only person in whom he could confide about her. Paul averred that for him the main thing was still not the sex but just being with her. The same with her, he went on; in fact, she didn't seem to want sex that much, and was more concerned about making him happy in other ways.

Richard again reflected that Paul seemed to have gained the relationship-security he had sought for so long. He had settled for companionship of a mainly non-sexual kind, and had not made large sexual demands because nothing in his experience had encouraged them. Richard recalled Paul's words about the scarcity of relationship-chances for someone like himself, and felt more strongly than ever that in this sphere Paul had made the right decision. He had taken what circumstances had offered, and had not looked either side of that offering. He had known all too well he was not the same kind of person as Harry, who had such a wide field of play.

Richard then thought about his own situation. Retracing earlier thoughts, he felt it true to say that for him there was a field to play, one much narrower than Harry's, yet broader than Paul's. On the other hand, a field was only possibilities, whereas he had the certainty of Pina's feelings for him. Another certainty he possessed was his sense of affinity with her, the like of which he had felt with no other woman, not even Helga. Should he perhaps settle for these sure and unequivocal things, and not look beyond them to the possibility of a relationship which, while containing sexual excitement, might lack them? The question hovered in his mind for a few moments, and he was tempted to answer 'yes', but he knew that finally he could not. Sexual gratification he must have. This gave relevance to whatever other features a relationship contained.

He replied to Paul, telling him about Portugal in general and his teaching in particular. But he did not mention Pina because he did not want to give him the false impression that he was having a sexual relationship with someone; and because he knew that, to avoid creating that impression, he would have to explain a number of things which he did not want to go into.

As he posted the letter, he found himself wondering how long his correspondence with Paul would last. Paul, now that he had the support he had longed for, might completely give up intellectual questing; and if that happened, a gulf would open up between them.

"Oh, Richard," called Simpson from his office door.

"Yes?" turning.

"Can I see you a moment?"

Richard went over.

"Richard, have you reported yet to the P.I.D.E.?"

Richard remembered he hadn't, and at the same time recalled Simpson's giving him the address. "No, I'm afraid not."

"You have to do it within three months of arrival, as you were told. You need to take your passport and your employment contract with you."

"Yes, I'll go as soon as I can."

"I'm asking," said Simpson, "because most of the other staff have already been, and I wouldn't…" pausing with a slight smile, "want to see you get yourself into any sort of trouble."

"Or the school, either," Richard couldn't resist replying.

"That's a secondary consideration, of course," still with the smile.

Later, Richard asked Roger if he had reported to the P.I.D.E. yet.

"No. Why, has Simpson collared you about it?"

"Yes, this morning."

"Well, he did me too. Apparently, if we don't report within the three month period, we might get deported. And the school might be heavily fined."

"Hence Simpson's concern."

"Exactly."

They decided to report together and fixed a date: an afternoon later that week, when neither was teaching.

The P.I.D.E. headquarters was in the centre of town, and they took a tram. As usual, youths held on to the back of the vehicle and had a free ride – laughing, shouting. Richard reflected that their merriment showed complete ignorance of the grim nature of the political situation in their country, one they might only begin to understand when called up into the armed forces to take part in the colonial wars now being waged in Africa.

Roger nudged his arm. "I think this is the stop."

They got off, and Richard saw the name of the road they were looking for, high up on the wall on the other side of the street.

The P.I.D.E. building was smaller than he had expected: a two-storey, long edifice in rococo style; pleasant-looking, Richard reflected with a sense of irony, like some of the banks and offices he had seen.

At the entrance, two uniformed policemen were posted. Inside, there was a reception area, longer than it was wide, lit by harshly bright fluorescent strips in the ceiling. Along one side of the area, stretching the length of it, was a white-marble counter; behind it stood female receptionists. Behind them were a number of doors of dark brown wood. The sight of the women led Richard to consider the contrast between this female element, at the periphery of the organisation, and the brutal male element, at the organisation's centre.

He and Roger went up to the counter. One of the receptionists, a rather short woman with jet-black hair and a sallow complexion, asked "Si?" without smiling.

"Ingles," replied Roger.

"English?" she echoed. "You are visitors?"

Roger than explained why they had come. She asked for their passports and work contracts, took them and then went through the door behind her. As they waited, Richard saw, further up the counter, a tall thin man in a light-blue suit emerge from one of the doors, ask a receptionist something, and then go back in. This man, thought Richard, was part of what the P.I.D.E. was essentially about; he would connect with another man in an office far from public view; and he in turn would connect with another. Somewhere along this chain would be the interrogators, torturers and even murderers who were an inevitable feature of a secret police system. But today, Roger and himself would encounter only female receptionists.

The woman with the sallow complexion returned. Still without the trace of a smile, she told them that everything was all right with their documents, which had now been date-stamped.

They must, she added, report again within three months, and continue to do so for as long as they were in the country.

Outside in the street, Roger said, "Well, that went off fairly smoothly. I suppose as long as your papers are in order, you're okay."

"Yes, for us it's all right. But not for plenty of other people – the ones you never see."

"No, I suppose not." He then glanced at his watch. "Look, I've arranged to meet Tessa in town, in about an hour. What are you doing now?"

Roger's words suggested to Richard that his mind had now moved past the subject of the P.I.D.E. Richard answered, "I think I'll go back to the flat."

"Well, got time for a quick cup of coffee?"

"All right."

They crossed to a small cafe on the other side of the street. Warmed by the afternoon sunlight, Richard again thought about his position as a free person in a society in which there were many who were unfree. He had an impulse to communicate this to Roger, but then heard him say, "You know. I'll have a beer instead of coffee. It's so damned hot."

"I'll have the same," deciding not to voice the subject.

CHAPTER THREE

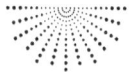

When Richard spoke to Pina after their next lesson, he told her about his visit to the P.I.D.E.

"It is curious," she said, "I have never had to go into that building. I have seen it only from the outside."

"From where, funnily enough, it looks quite attractive."

"Yes," with a slight smile. But then her brow furrowed. "It is very different from the prisons where so many people are kept because they have protested against the government."

"Where are the prisons?"

"In different parts of the country, but not in the cities. In places where few people go."

"Have you seen any of them?"

"Yes, from a distance. Travelling by car, with friends. And I know someone who was imprisoned, in the north of the country. He was beaten and tortured."

"Is he free now?"

"Yes. He works as an architect. But he is no longer participating in politics. The beatings and the torture weakened him, in his spirit as well as in his body. He now accepts the political situation, and lives quietly with his family."

"But he must have been very active before his arrest."

"He was."

After a moment, he said, "In a way, it's sad." But at the same time, he felt he understood how physical violence, prolonged and excessive, could break a person's spirit, and he did not think that he himself could stand up under it for very long. He recalled being bullied at school, but realised this was nothing compared with what Pina's friend had experienced.

"Yes," replied Pina. "This feeling of defeat – it happens to many."

"But I suppose there are others who are never deterred, no matter what's done to them."

"Of course."

He tried to imagine what it must be like to be one of those: to have proved your courage beyond question. He felt such proof was not his own possession. His train of thought was interrupted by Pina saying, "If only our political problems could be solved. Then there would be no need for protest, or the P.I.D.E., or the political prisons."

Richard nodded, glad to concentrate on these larger issues rather than on thoughts of his own inadequacy. "You said," he began, "that the wars in Africa have been going on for ten years."

"Yes. Longer than your government's war in Kenya in the 1950s."

He looked at her quickly. Her eyes showed both seriousness and a trace of amusement. She was reminding him, he realised, that Britain too had fought colonial wars in Africa, and not so long ago.

"You do not mind that I say this?" she asked.

"No, of course not. You're quite right about Kenya."

"I know these things from my reading."

He found himself thinking of Helga, and of his discussion with her about British imperialism. He asked, "Then you've read some history?"

"Quite a lot. Much of it is brutal,"

"You mean the empires, the wars and the conquests?"

She nodded.

"Yes," he agreed. He thought again about his self-doubts on the subject of courage, but now in relation to those people who deliberately committed brutalities. They had had no problems in launching into decisive action; they had not been plagued by self-doubts. Nor--the thought suddenly came to him-- could they have experienced the paralysing sense of the sky's emptiness that he had known. It would have been better if they had encountered all these problems; perhaps then they would not have acted as they had.

"Yes," he repeated, "there have always been people who have just gone ahead and done the most terrible things, for wealth and power." Still thinking about the sky's emptiness, his mind moved to his conviction that there was no God, and he added, "And nothing has ever stopped them except other people."

"Only other people?" asked Pina.

"Why do you say 'only'?"

After a moment, she answered, "Well, perhaps there is something more."

"God, do you mean?"

"Perhaps."

"I don't think so."

"But you don't know."

"No, of course I don't. I can only have an opinion. Like everybody else. But that opinion is what I have to act on. I have no other basis for action…" He fell silent. He did not want to become overly-assertive; partly because he wasn't sure it was appropriate for him to talk about action when, in his view, he had done very little; and partly because he again wanted to get away from the subject of himself and back to larger topics.

Before he could say anything on the latter, Pina replied, "Yes, I suppose so. We have to act on our beliefs, even if we cannot be sure they are right."

"And what are yours?"

She exhaled, taking his hand in both hers. He accepted the gesture as an aspect of the rapport between them. She replied, "I do not know, Richard. I wish I did."

" But you talk about God."

"That is mostly – what is your word? – my upbringing. My parents are Catholic."

"Well, it's good that you've recognised that." Then, "And about what we were saying before: I don't think there's anything to stop evil except people."

"And what about – I am trying to think of the right word – the origination of evil?"

"The origin?" realising the Portuguese word was 'originaçao'. "That's people too. So, it's people against people."

As he spoke, he felt sure of himself in the sense of being certain of the points he was making. But, when he paused, he wished he could feel as sure of himself in other respects.

"This," said Pina, "is what I have sometimes thought."

"I can't see any other way of looking at it. If you can beat the people who do the evil, you can beat evil... But I'm not really the one to be talking about this. You've had more experience of evil than I have."

"Perhaps. But I have not thought about it in the way you have."

"Then," he smiled, "we'll have to combine your experience with my thought." 'And hopefully,' he said to himself, 'my future action.'

"But, Richard, what about something you have already seen – the baracas? That is a result of injustice."

"Yes, what about it?"

"Would you like to see another?"

He nodded.

"It is called 'Madre de Deus'."

"Mother of God?"

"It is a strange name for a slum, I know. This is one of the biggest in Lisbon. Another big one is near Benfica football stadium."

"Shall we go next Sunday?"

She nodded.

CHAPTER FOUR

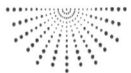

WHEN RICHARD AWOKE ON SUNDAY MORNING, HE SAW, THROUGH THE window, a thin but steady drizzle, and recalled that during the night he had been awakened by the sound of heavy rain. The sky was bleary-grey. When he left the house, he realised he had underestimated the coldness of the air; he went back and put on a thick vest under his shirt, jacket and raincoat.

Approaching the bus stop where he had arranged to meet Pina, he saw someone about her height, an umbrella covering head and shoulders. Then he glanced down, and recognised the shortness and thickness of the lower part of her legs. Briefly, the wish that he could desire her returned to him. He walked over, a gentle smile on his lips, for when she would see him.

"Pina."

The umbrella swung round and her wide face was on his. Her eyes momentarily glowed, but then their lids touched together, their light slackened, and her lips parted in a smile: "Richard. You are early." He sensed she had controlled an initial surge of desire on seeing him.

"Am I?"

"See," holding up her wrist, its small-dialled watch indicating the time. Again, he noted the black hair on her lower forearm. "Ah, yes," he acknowledged.

The bus arrived. Soon it was climbing through the suburbs. Rain streaked the windows and people hurried along the pavements, often sharing umbrellas, gesticulating as they talked. There were frequent gaps in the pavement; brown earth, now moistening to mud, filling the space between the paving stones. Several cafes were below street-level and badly lit. Some of them sold smoked fish, and the smoke drifted from the charcoal-braziers just outside the doors, up to street level, thinning against the wind. On a number of street corners, shoe-shiners, from pre-adolescents to old men, busily plied their trade under cover of shop and cafe awnings, sitting not far from the kerbs and the rain-clogged gutters. People spat, as usual, but the asphalt did not have its usual viscous patches because of the rain.

The bus pulled into the terminus.

"Now, we go this way," said Pina. They walked between two high, old buildings and came out into a clearing.

A mass of pale brown extended about half a mile to their left and right, and about forty feet down, in a ridged slope, to flat ground at the bottom. On the far side of the flatness, there was another slope of about the same height, but with wider ridges. On the lower ridges and at the bottom of the slope, there were shacks. Smoke, from what Richard assumed were indoor stoves, trailed up into the rain mist. A stream of rain flowed through a natural ditch which stretched from one end of the flat ground mist to the other, fed by channels from the slopes.

Richard and Pina descended the slope, treading along a line of wooden planks which were placed close together but did not actually meet end to end. The lower they went, the louder the sound of the stream became. The water moved fast, with cross-ripples and twists to the current. As he watched it, Pina said, "Sometimes, when it rains hard for a long time, the river stays for weeks."

And not just in the ditch, he realised. They crossed the flat ground to the other side, drawing nearer the shacks.

But gradually, the rain slackened; then stopped. The sun appeared.

From one of the shacks, a woman emerged with a bucket, and walked toward a tap fixed at the end of a piece of piping that stuck out of the ground at a slight angle. In places, old shoes and discarded bits of clothing were trodden into the mud. From another shack, a small boy of six or seven appeared, wearing only a vest which was too short for him, and began climbing up a rubbish pile. Higher up, clucking chickens bobbed along a ridge, and a dog barked.

"This," said Pina, "is how they live. Every day. Every year."

From several other shacks, both on the flat ground and on the ridges, a number of boys emerged, about 11 or 12 years old. They wore torn shirts and shorts and heavy, worn-looking shoes which seemed to have no laces or tongues. One boy carried a large ball. The group crowded together on the flatness, then divided into two teams and began a game of football.

They played rough, pulling at each other's shirts and arms as they vied for the ball, which barely bounced as it hit the muddy surface of the ground.

On the side-lines, a boy sat with his head lowered, turning the heels of his bare feet into the surface of a patch of mud. Richard had previously noticed him come out of one of the shacks after the others, and go over to where he was now.

"Something is wrong, perhaps," said Pina. She then went over to the boy. She bent down and he looked up. At first, he kept lowering his head as she spoke, but then he grinned at something she said, and began to talk, still turning his heel in the ground. She stroked his spiky, unwashed hair while she listened.

Returning to Richard, she said: "He told me they do not let him play with them because he has no boots. He says he does not like to wear boots or shoes."

"Has he got any?"

"Yes, some old boots, like theirs, but he no longer wears them."

"Maybe it's just as well that they don't let him play. He'd injure his feet without boots."

"He said he wanted to play in goal, which he is good at."

"Well, yes, there he wouldn't need boots as much."

"But it seems the others did not want him to play át áll. They did not want him to play even when he wore boots. He says they have been this way with him for long time." Then, "Ah, if it is true, it is very bád of thém."

On the last words, her voice rose in pitch. Then, meeting his eyes, she smiled to herself, "Ah, but I am very Latin, Richard."

"Yes, you are," wanting to hug her plumpness and press a near-brotherly kiss to her cheek.

"Perhaps too Latin," she added, with a close-and-open of her eyelids that was part of a slight head-turn.

"No," he insisted, "never that." At the same time. he was wondering about the boy. Why was it that the other boys were apparently against him? Was it the case that, even here, under the simplest and most primitive conditions, there were complex differences between people, just as in the more sophisticated situations he was familiar with: differences, moreover, which emerged as early as childhood?

They walked on, up the slope. This, like the first one, had a system of planks. At the top, there was a hillock, and in front of it two very old houses, each three storeys high, their walls cracked. In between them stood a tall, dead palm tree.

Sounds of activity came from behind the hillock. Richard asked, "What do you think is going on?"

"I think I know. But let us go and see."

They walked round the bottom of the hill. On the other side, men of all ages were ranged up the slope digging, joking, shouting. One man wore a construction helmet. They were clearing away a layer of rain-made mud that threatened to slide down onto their shacks. While the men worked, small children were throwing mud balls, underhand, up into the air to see who could get the highest. Old women sat in chairs in front of their shacks, now and then gesticulating toward the work and calling out. Some younger women were going up and down the slope, supplying the men with chunks of bread.

"The mud," said Pina, "is always a danger after rain."

"Yes." Then, "Here, there's so much going on among the adults, but in other parts of the baracas – nothing."

Pina nodded. "In some parts, people do things together; in other parts, no. Even during the floods, some people do repair work by themselves, others do it in groups."

Again, he thought about the boy debarred from football. 'Differences even here': the thought echoed in his mind as they walked along, in the direction they had come. He realised he should not have expected anything else; there was no more reason to assume unanimity among the poor than among the better-off.

As they re-traced their stops across the flat area, he saw that the match was still going on, but that the boy without shoes had gone. They ascended the final slope, and came out onto the roadway.

Pina said, "So much mud! So much dampness! There is a lot of tuberculosis in these slums."

"Yes, I can imagine."

"But, you know, these people do not get good treatment. It is mostly the rich who go into hospitals. Most of the poor must go on living where they are, taking medicines which the hospitals give them. The hospitals only ask to see them from time to time."

"You know a lot about the situation."

"Because of my work in the government welfare office."

"Ah yes," recalling her telling him about this. "It must give you a very wide picture." A far wider one, he thought, than did his work at the school, where he met only the better-off, none of whom ever mentioned the slums. He now wondered how many of them knew about the poverty but did not give it a second thought, and how many simply did not know.

His mind now moved to the view that, despite the fact that

there were complex problems in the baracas as everywhere else, the basic issue of poverty remained paramount.

They took the bus back into town, and were soon in the midst of tall office buildings, wide avenues, shops and restaurants.

"This is like another world," he said, feeling uncomfortable at being fortunate enough to be able to move so easily from one social context to another.

"Yes, another world," Pina concurred.

When they got off the bus, they strolled through the crowded streets, her arm in his. They stopped at a cafe to have a cup of coffee; and again he felt uneasy about his good fortune.

Afterwards, they continued walking. The sun was now very bright, and the sky completely blue. As they strolled along, looking in shop windows, he noticed the feeling of discomfort receding, and thought this due to the cumulative effect of being among familiar things again.

At around five o'clock, they had dinner in a small restaurant. He had noticed, in the previous hour or so, that Pina had said little, in contrast to earlier. Now, as they ate, she frequently looked down at her plate. Eventually, he asked her, "Is there anything you want to tell me?"

She glanced at him, down again, then laid her hand on his. "It is difficult to tell."

"You can try."

After a moment, she said, "Well, last night, in bed. I…" pausing, bringing the fingertips of her other hand to her forehead.

He felt he knew what she meant. "Masturbated?"

"Yes. That is the word." She raised her eyes. Then, in a murmur, "You."

He felt slightly embarrassed, and slightly flattered, but also saw her sexual loneliness. He was reminded of Helga's similar admission.

"I did not," she went on, "say that to make you pity me."

"I know."

She lowered her head again. In the silence, he thought of his own experience of masturbation, and that of other people who faced the night alone and confronted the choice of whether or not to trump reality by creating, through self-stimulus, a deep, vigorous, tender world – but one which evaporated with orgasm. He knew that the temptation was to seize the moment and clasp the make-believe, at the inevitable cost of void and pain later.

He gently squeezed her fingers. She returned the pressure. Briefly, he reflected that, under other circumstances, these gestures would signify mutual physical attraction.

She looked up and asked, "Do you masturbate?"

He nodded. She did not say anything. She would know, he concluded, that she was not his stimulus. Their hands stayed together: a kind of bridge, he felt, across their sexual differences.

With the return of silence, he considered the fact that, for all people of sensitivity, sexual fulfilment was sought as the deepest release from isolation, one which neither he nor she had yet found. That release, he realised, must also be sought by many living in extreme poverty.

"I think," she said eventually, "that a lot of people must masturbate."

"Yes. But no one likes to admit it. Masturbation is a huge, undeclared fact."

After a moment, she replied, "I am glad we can talk about it like this."

Recalling his relationship with Paul, he responded, "So am I," again squeezing her fingers.

Through the window, he could see the sun was setting. Soon it would be time to take Pina home; and then they would inevitably go their separate ways into the night.

The waiter placed their bill at the edge of the table.

"Richard, this time, let me pay."

"But…"

"Please, let me," earnest insistence in her eyes. "I have enjoyed so much our talking together."

She opened her purse and gave the waiter the money.

Outside, the sky near the rooftops was orange: the brief orange that would soon fade into black. They boarded the bus and, as they sat down, she put her arm in his. He accepted this gesture as he had her previous one of laying her hand on his.

The bus arrived at her stop and they got off. By now the orange was fading and, above it, a few stars were visible.

His eyes lowered to hers, and saw they were looking into his with a soft, open light. Then the light changed slightly, her eyebrows lifted, and she said, "It is time for me to go now," with gentle resignation in her voice.

"Okay," he replied, and quickly kissed her forehead.

He would, he said, see her at tomorrow's lesson. He raised his arm and waved as she walked toward the end of the street. Then he turned and headed the other way, under the street lamps. The night air was warm, and he felt a sudden impulse to go drinking; but then it seemed to him that moving indiscriminately from bar to bar would violate the spirit in which the earlier part of the day had been spent. That spirit he wanted to preserve. He took the tram back to the flat.

CHAPTER FIVE

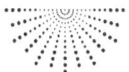

When Richard got home, he found Roger in the sitting-room eating a sandwich. Licking his fingertips. Roger smiled: "Hello. Been anywhere interesting?"

"I certainly have," and said he had been to see the slum area of Madre de Deus. He briefly described its main features.

When he had finished, Roger responded, "Yes… it's tough, I know." Then, "Who took you there?"

"One of my students. Her name is Pina."

"Am I allowed to ask if she's attractive?"

"That's changing the subject," with a smile, not wanting to talk about this, yet not wanting to say so bluntly.

" Yes, of course it is," replied Roger. "Okay, I'll change to a different subject. Tessa's now found a place of her own. Quite a good furnished room."

"Oh, where?"

"Near the harbour. I can get the tram straight down."

He took another bite of his sandwich and put the remainder down on the plate he had at his side. "Couple of other things I wanted to mention. Simpson's decided to cancel that dance at the school he was planning – apparently it was too much hassle to get permission from the authorities to hold a public event."

Momentarily, Richard thought of Jennie, and her work on the posters.

"The other thing," Roger continued, "is that Tessa and I were in the town centre the other night and we saw the new teacher – I forget his name – getting into a taxi with two young chaps. I don't think they were his students."

"You mean Daniel?"

"Yeh, Daniel. Anyway," with a grin, "one of the chaps had his arm around Daniel's waist. Are you thinking what I'm thinking?"

"Probably." Richard then described how he had seen Daniel pick up a young man at the Cafe Suisse.

"Then he hasn't wasted much time," said Roger.

This comment reminded Richard of the impression he had previously had of Daniel's sexual self-confidence.

"I wonder," Roger went on, "what it's like to be queer?"

Richard, noting the use of the word 'queer' rather than 'homosexual,' replied, "Yes, it's a very different experience from ours. It must be difficult in the early years, around puberty, to know you're different from the majority, and to have to hide the fact."

"Um, I hadn't thought of it that way before."

Richard assumed that Daniel had known such difficulty at the time of puberty, and now thought again about his self-confidence, connected as that was with his promiscuity. "Maybe," he said, "the way he carries on now is partly a reaction against the fears and secretiveness of those early years. And, if the secret got out then, maybe he was laughed at, or pushed around."

"It's all getting a bit too complicated," said Roger, finishing the last part of his sandwich. "I'm turning in. I've got to get up early tomorrow to do lesson preparation I should have done today."

A few weeks later, Richard met Pina before the lesson, as usual, and she told him about a political meeting that was to take place at the University the following Sunday. It had been organised by students from Lisbon and Coimbra to discuss protest activity against the government's colonial wars in Mozambique and Angola.

"Would you like to go?" she asked.

He recalled Simpson's warning to the teachers about the consequences of getting involved in political agitation; but then he nodded. This, he felt, was a risk worth taking. They arranged to meet at the bus stop near her home.

Once again, he saw her from a distance as he approached. He experienced a combination of feelings which had now become familiar: nearness to her in mind and spirit, far-ness from her in terms of physical desire. It was a complex, difficult combination that he knew he would have to live with,

She held out her cheek to be kissed, a gesture which, he realised, was made in full awareness of the fact that he did not desire her. He touched his lips to the rosy-coloured plumpness.

"We must hurry, Richard. The meeting starts in one hour."

They walked a couple of streets, then took a tram in a direction Richard did not know. The vehicle was almost empty and they sat at the back. She told him she had been given instructions on how to find the meeting place at the University, and added that she herself had been a student there, but had had to give up her studies because her parents did not have enough money.

"We do not receive money from the government to study, as I think you do in England."

"Yes, we do. We get grants, the amount depending on our parents' income. We have a pretty well developed welfare system."

"It is because your country is wealthier. If it were like Portugal, it would not have such a system."

"That's right." He had not thought of this before.

"And," Pina went on, "it is wealthier partly because it had a much bigger empire than Portugal – so more materials for its economy."

Again, this was a new thought for him. He recalled the

previous things she had said about British imperialism. "More of your reading?" he smiled.

"Yes. I have been looking at some things by Marx. He has a lot to say about empires."

"I should read him too," feeling he should have done so already.

The tram continued to move through streets he did not recognise, and at last came to a high point in the city, with lots of open space and a view of the harbour. To the left, Richard saw a group of white-coloured buildings in spacious grounds. The main one had a frontage of ten columns, spaced across the top of a stone step-way.

"Do you like," asked Pina, "the design of the University?"

"Yes." but he couldn't help contrasting it with the baracas, and he remembered what she had said about having to give up her studies. "Yes," he continued, "but it's a place only for those who can afford it."

"I know, but some are people of good social consciousness. You will see."

The grounds were quiet, with only a few people going in and out of the buildings. Pina led the way, and they crossed a long, diagonal pathway between green lawns, which took them away from the larger buildings. Then they came to a very big open space, with soccer pitches and a running track. It was deserted. In the middle of it was a long, bungalow-type building, with trees dotted round it.

Pointing to the building Pina said, "That is the sports dressing rooms."

He glanced at her.

"Yes," she went on, "that is where the meeting will be."

Gradually they approached the building. About 200 yards from it, they passed one of the trees, and Richard saw a young man standing behind it. His face turned to Pina in a smile of recognition. In one hand he held a walkie-talkie. Pina said something to him in Portuguese, after which he glanced quickly at Richard, than nodded.

Pina and Richard continued on their way. "He is," she said, "oh, I do not know the word in English."

"A look-out."

" 'Look-out'. Yes."

"He is well-placed. He can see a long way in several directions."

"That is why the dressing-rooms have been chosen."

As they walked round one side of the building, Richard saw another young man behind a tree, again about 200 yards off, looking in a different direction. He too was holding something, and Richard took it to be another walkie-talkie.

At the entrance to the building, on the far side, stood a third man with a walkie-talkie. Richard now fully comprehended the communications network. Pina spoke to the man, again in Portuguese, and he turned to Richard, holding out his hand.

"Pleased to meet you. I think you will find the meeting interesting."

Noting the man's apparent fluency in English, Richard replied, "I'm certain I will."

The man opened the door, and Richard and Pina entered a long room with yellow-tiled floor and walls, and wooden benches along the length of it. On the walls were clothes hooks. People were sitting on the benches talking together in groups, and some looked up at the new arrivals. At the far end of the room was a transparent plastic-type curtain, which Richard assumed indicated the shower area.

A young woman came over to Pina. They hugged each other and began talking quickly in Portuguese. Amid the talk, Pina turned her head to Richard, and so did the woman, Richard guessed that Pina was telling her something about him. Then some other people came over, and she introduced them all to him.

"Attençao, attençao," called a voice from about halfway down the room. A man was standing up, with one foot on the bench, his hands cupped round his mouth.

"The meeting is starting now," Pina whispered to Richard. "This is the man who has led previous ones."

The man began speaking in Portuguese, and although he went quite fast, Richard picked up enough to understand that there would be a series of speakers.

The first speaker was a tall, thin man who articulated his points fairly slowly. With Pina's help, Richard was able to understand almost everything he said. In what seemed to him a curiously quiet voice, the man advocated armed violence as the only way of removing the government and putting an end to its imperialist policies. He urged the formation of urban guerrilla groups to begin a campaign of incendiarism and bombing. The time for talking was over, he contended; the only thing the government understood was force.

There was some scattered applause. Richard asked Pina, "Have you heard him speak before?"

"Yes. He has some support among the students."

"He speaks with such a quiet voice, for someone who advocates violence."

"But I have heard him shout too, at people who did not agree with him. First he smiled, then he shouted."

The second speaker got up. He argued that the protest movement should not resort to violence except under extreme provocation. Fighting was a last option and should not be chosen unless all other methods failed.

Richard noted the contrast between the two speakers – not only in viewpoint but also in vocal delivery, the latter articulating in a swift and vigorous manner.

The man went on to say that the less the movement attracted the attention of the authorities, the better – for the present at least. The lower its profile, the more freedom and leeway it would have. It could get on with very useful activities: for example, secretly raising money to help the insurgents in Mozambique and Angola.

He sat down, to widespread applause. Richard was pleased to see this argument better received than the previous one, since he thought it made more sense. Pina was clapping vigorously. A third speaker got up.

Suddenly the door was flung open, to reveal the man with the walkie-talkie who had shaken hands with him on arrival. "Police! Police!" the man called out, and gestured for people to leave immediately.

Pina said to Richard, "Someone must have informed to the police," and grasped his hand tightly.

People were being ushered out of the door. Outside, the man with the walkie-talkie was pointing his arm for people to run in the direction away from the campus. In the distance, Richard could hear shouts from rough, deep voices. As people started running, Richard looked at Pina, and she at him. Still holding hands, they took off.

A boom-sound split the air, and some dirt was thrown up about twenty yards to their left. 'They're firing at us', Richard realised, breathing too heavily to say anything to Pina, but she shot an anxious glance at him which told him she realised it too. Ahead, at the edge of the open space were some trees, and Richard was counting the seconds till they reached them; the trees would provide cover from gunfire.

Just as they passed into the shadow cast by the tree branches, they heard another gunshot, but did not see where the bullet had hit. Ahead, through the spaces between the tree trunks, was a downhill slope with a main road at the bottom, 'If only,' he thought, "we can get to that road'. They came out of the trees, into the full glare of sunlight; and, as they went down the slope, he felt his breathing ease. His arm was stretched backward, because Pina's pace was slower than his, and he looked back at her; her face was flushed deeply, and her eyes showed strain and fear. He now had enough breath to say to her, "Just a little further."

The road got nearer and he saw a tram approaching, with a second one not far behind. There had been no more shots, he realised. The slope steepened, hardening the impact of his feet on the grass. Then the ground started to level out. Everyone in the group made for the first tram as it slowed toward the stop.

Richard saw there were too many people to get on the first one, and he swerved leftward, clutching Pina's hand tighter, for the second. Several other people did the same. The tram halted and they boarded. Trying to catch his breath, he fumbled in his pocket for money to pay for the two tickets, and produced the necessary coins. He and Pina moved further down into the tram. Looking through the window, he could see no sign of the police on the slope. The tram jolted and began to move. He swallowed.

The other people were still breathing heavily. He noted that no one said anything, and saw that this was because they did not want to draw attention to themselves; if they did, and if the other passengers were to realise what had happened, the tram might be stopped. Pina, having just caught her breath, was looking up at him with a smile, but remained silent.

The tram rumbled on, entering the harbour area; as Richard's ear became attuned to the hum of conversation from the seated passengers, he realised that the danger had passed. But why had the police not pursued them?

A whisper passed along the line. Pina conveyed the message to him: they were all to get off at the stop after next.

When that came, they all stepped out of the tram-shadow into the sunlit street. Richard saw no sign of the first tram and assumed it had taken a different route. One of the people in the group indicated that they should move over to a deserted space by the harbour wall. They did.

Richard then learned what had happened earlier. One of the students said that, with the second gunshot, he had seen a young man fall and another stop; and he assumed that the police had stopped pursuing them because they were content to have one, perhaps two captives. Also, they didn't like a public show of violence, which is what would have happened if they had continued their pursuit to the main road. They would interrogate whomever they caught, to find out as much as they could.

Richard wondered about the physical condition of the fallen student, and whether he would have had the courage to stop if he himself had seen him fall. He tried to imagine the interrogation process. Also, he was worried at the possibility of Pina's name coming up at the questioning. He asked her if many of the students at the meeting knew her name.

"No, only some, and they all reached the trams. Why do you ask?"

Feeling relief, he explained.

"It is all right," she smiled. "I am safe." She stroked his hand with hers, "But think about the one who has been caught," her brow furrowing.

"Yes," again trying to picture the interrogation situation.

"I hope the person who fell is not badly wounded."

"Will they question him even if he is?"

"Well, if he is very badly hurt, they will first give him hospital treatment, to ensure he remains alive. But then they will interrogate. If they have the other person, the one who stopped, they will interrogate straightaway."

"And," Richard asked, "use torture?" recalling what she had previously told him about the man she knew who had retreated from political activity after being tortured.

"If he refuses to speak, yes."

He lowered his head, knowing he could do nothing to prevent it. When he looked up again, he saw that the other students were dispersing. The young woman who had greeted Pina in the dressing rooms came over, and they talked for a few moments in Portuguese; then she said goodbye to her, wiping a tear from her eye. Some other people also came over and exchanged a few words with Pina before leaving.

Richard asked her if the students had any idea of who told the police.

"No, but they say they will go on arranging meetings, for the protest movement to continue. They say they will also try and find out what happened to the student who fell, and the other one."

As she spoke, he reflected that he had just been involved with her in what had been the most dangerous moment of his life. Finding this appropriate, he smiled with a sense that their relationship was deep and flexible enough to accommodate a very wide range of experiences. "We deserve," he said, "a cup of coffee after all that."

She grinned, nodding. He took her arm and they went toward the crowds and the shops. As with their visit to the baracas, he felt a little uncomfortable at being able to move from a harsh situation to an easy one; but now tiredness and nervous strain reconciled him to it.

CHAPTER SIX

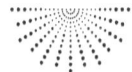

Roger's face went into a comic grimace as he lifted the pot off the stove and poured into Richard's coffee cup. "O-oh, if Simpson ever found out about it…"

"He won't."

"But you know what would happen if he did."

"Termination of contract," bringing the cup to his lips.

"Anyway," lighting a cigarette, "with Pina you certainly get around, don't you?"

"I suppose I do, yes."

Roger glanced quickly at him, drew on his cigarette, and asked, "Can I repeat the question I asked before?"

"About," Richard recalled, "whether she's attractive?"

Roger nodded.

After a moment, Richard replied, "Well, let me explain."

As he spoke, he tried to be as concise as possible. Roger listened with a concentrated expression. Then, "Um. It's sort of an unusual situation."

"And one difficult to find your bearings in, at first."

After a moment, Roger asked: "What will you do?"

"Go on seeing her. She knows the position, so it shouldn't cause problems."

"Actually," said Roger, "I know a bit about this from personal experience. You know, being fancied by women I didn't fancy. But I wasn't involved with them the way you are with Pina. I find that if I don't fancy someone, that's more or less that. I'm just not interested, but with you it's different."

"With me it's different," echoed Richard.

Later, Richard reflected on this contrast with Roger. He knew that Roger's attitude was widespread, among both men and women, and he recalled the responses, to himself and others, of many of the girls at his old school.

He was sitting in the cafe near the school, having some lunch. He had just finished a heavy morning's teaching and was feeling a little tired. Looking up from his plate, he saw Daniel come in. Daniel stood at the entrance for a moment, looked round the room, then saw him. After a moment, he began to walk toward him,

"Can I join you?" eyes at a slight angle.

"Of course."

Daniel drew the chair away from the table and then pulled it underneath him. He raised his eyes slowly to Richard, smiled, and asked if he used this restaurant much.

Noting Daniel's caution. Richard replied, "Now and then. Sometimes I don't eat at all at lunch-times."

Daniel then said he'd only been here once before, and picked up the menu. He held it in both hands, quite close to his face, and looked at it intently. To Richard, his gestures seemed exaggerated, and he wondered if he was deeply uneasy. He was mindful of the fact that this was their first conversation together.

"Yes. I'll have that," said Daniel, and turned his head to attract the waiter's attention. After he had given his order, his eyes went back again slowly to Richard.

Richard asked, "And how have you been settling in?"

"Oh, fine," quickly.

"Been getting to know Lisbon?"

"Yes. Interesting city."

The waiter came with Daniel's food, and he began eating. As he swallowed, the movement of his Adam's apple was conspicuous.

Two young men entered. As they passed by the table, Daniel glanced up; his eyes becoming keen with interest. Then he saw Richard looking at him; his eyes lowered, and he continued eating. Richard noted that the two men went to their table, neither showing any interest in Daniel.

Still looking down, Daniel smiled, in a different way to before. When he raised his eyes, they had, for the first time, an amused light. "So," he said, "you saw. That sort of breaks the ice."

Richard realised that, when Daniel had caught his look, his own eyes must have revealed more than he realised. For a moment, he did not know what to say. Then, "Okay, so I did." He added, "I also saw you one day at the Praca Rossio."

"Were you shocked?" eyes still with the amused light.

"No."

"Many would be."

"I'm not prejudiced."

"And I can't stand those who are," eyes losing their amusement, "I like to make fools of them whenever I get the chance."

Richard remembered the thoughts about Daniel's past which he had expressed to Roger. "Because," he asked, "of the trouble they've given you?"

Daniel's eyes rested on his. "That's right. You've seen the sort of thing I mean?"

"No, but I can imagine it." He decided he would now tell Daniel what Roger had said about seeing him get into a taxi with two youths.

Daniel listened, and replied, "Well, do you think I'm promiscuous?"

"It's difficult to avoid that conclusion."

"If I am," Daniel went on, "the reason is, I suppose, that I want to be rebellious."

Richard again recalled his earlier thoughts. "Because of the way you were treated in the past?"

Daniel nodded.

After a moment, Richard asked: "But isn't there a danger – that you'll miss love?"

"I don't think about love," Daniel retorted. "Only pleasure. I've got a strong appetite."

Richard remembered his own lustful tendencies, but still asked, "Shouldn't you think about it?"

Daniel exhaled, and said, just audibly, "Some time, perhaps, I will." Then, looking down, he put some food on his fork.

Richard felt that his words had made some impression on him, one which conflicted with his rebelliousness.

Leaving his fork on the side of his plate, Daniel looked up with a smile which, though slight, showed warmth. "Thanks, by the way."

"For what?"

"For using the word 'love'. That really proved you weren't prejudiced."

CHAPTER SEVEN

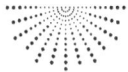

"Yes," said Pina, "the police did capture both."

"How did you find out?"

"Through contacts. The student organisation has many." Then, "The student who was shot is very ill in hospital. He was hit in the back. He may die."

"If he does, will the police be held responsible?"

"No, that does not happen."

Absorbing this point, Richard then asked, "What about the other student?"

"He has been interrogated. He was held at the Central Police Station, but has now been moved somewhere else. We are trying to find out where."

"Why do you think he was moved?"

"For worse interrogation. The police have special places, with special instruments."

Once again, Richard felt a sense of helplessness. He pressed Pina's plump hand. Her eyes showed that she knew his gesture sprang from anxiety. "We will," she said, "just have to wait." He nodded in silence.

"You must think." she went on, "that this is a terrible country."

"Well," finding himself curiously tempted to witticism, "it could stand some improvement."

She smiled. "Of course. But you should remember that your country is Portugal's oldest ally. That is the phrase that is always used."

"Something else I didn't know. How far does the friendship go back?"

"Hundreds of years. To when both countries were involved in the New World, and both were enemies of Spain."

"And is it still strong?"

"Strong enough for your government to say nothing about Portugal's wars in Angola and Mozambique."

"It seems," he said after a moment, "that so many things are interconnected, once you look into them. I'll have to look into them more."

"So will I."

"But you're ahead of me."

"I think that is because, in Portugal, we live under pressure. I have learned a lot because all the restrictions on us make us keener for knowledge."

"The whole population?"

"Well, some of us."

Pina told him that the wounded student had died.

"What," he asked, "will his parents do?"

"What can they do? There are no means of prosecuting the police."

"And of course you have no parliament, so there is no representative they can go to."

She shook her head, adding, "And no freedom of press. No newspaper would speak for the parents. They can share their grief and bitterness only with friends."

Silence followed. They both lowered their heads.

Eventually, Pina raised hers with, "Because there is nothing we can do for present, we should think about other things. Yes?"

"Yes," meeting her eyes. "I imagine awful things are going on in this country, and of course in other countries, all the time. If you knew and worried about them all, you'd be suffocated."

They began to talk about the weekend, and decided they would visit a nearby coastal area with high rocks called Praia da Rocha.

From the windy cliff-top, they looked down to the shore. Big rocks, in sprawling piles, broke the incoming waves.

He felt an impulse to go to the edge of the cliff and examine its gradient. "I'll just be a minute," he said, and went forward in a crouch.

"What are you doing?" she called, and he could detect anxiety in her voice.

He looked back. "I just want to see how steep the cliff is."

"But perhaps the earth is loose at the edge."

"Oh, probably not," but conscious he had not thought about this.

From where he was, he could see the cliff edge because the ground dipped before it. Still in a crouch, he stopped where the dip began. There was room to go forward, but he saw cracks in the dry earth. Dropping onto his knees, he reached forward and pushed against a crack nearest the edge. A slice of earth, a few inches wide and about a foot deep fell away. 'She was right,' he thought. Through the gap that was left, he looked down at the rock-face. It swelled outward, then dipped inward about 50 feet down, to come out again after about 30 feet, in slow-falling ridges to the beach below. Altogether, he judged the height to be about 150 feet.

He looked round and saw Pina's back turned to him. He did not call out but went over to her. When he touched his hand to her shoulder, she looked round at him.

"Why do you do such a thing?" she asked.

He realised she had been worried enough to avert her eyes.

"You could have fallen down" she went on, "the earth could have broken away, many things…" She was flushed now, talking very fast, her shoulders tightening at moments. Suddenly, she stopped. Then, quietly, "Anything could have happened, Richard,"

With a smile, he stroked her cheek. She smiled too, in a way he recognised as showing self-amusement. She put out her chin, in a parody of annoyance: "You are very bad."

"I know," going along with the parody, but also thinking about the protectiveness which had lain at the root of her anxiety: the protectiveness which was part of the love he could not reciprocate.

"Come," she said, "let us walk," putting her arm in his.

Cloud was packed in a near-level line across the sky, its whiteness brighter than the blue above it. On the crest of the cliff, they caught the full wind from the sea. Offshore stood a column of rock completely cut off from the land. Pointing to it, Richard said it was like a monument, and that it must be the result of hundreds or even thousands of years of erosion.

"Yes," she replied, "so much time that, in comparison, our lives are only a few seconds."

He looked at her, again struck by the way she had expressed herself. Her eyes, gazing out to sea, were pensive above the soft convex of her cheeks. He brought his hand to her cheek, brushing his fingertips against it. Her eyes turned to his, and she took his hand in hers. He smiled with the deep affection he continually felt for her, and then looked at the hand that held his; noting, as he had before, that it was as large as his.

"Yes," she said, "my hands are too big."

"But I have small hands for a man," perceiving that she had picked up his thought. Then, "Yours are bright and warm and capable hands."

"But I know they do not excite."

'No,' he silently agreed, seeing them as the hands of a homely, dedicated housewife.

"I now accept," she went on, "that they do not."

He nodded, then asked, "And at one time you didn't?"

"No. I used nail-polish – the silver kind. But it looked silly, so I removed it."

Again, he nodded.

The wind was blowing strongly now, and he shivered slightly.

"You are cold?" she asked.

"A little," realising she was no longer thinking about her hands.

"Then we will go down."

"But not if you want to stay up here. I don't mind,"

"No. It is warmer below."

Below, they came to the main road; it was shaded with tall trees that sieved the wind. Walking along arm in arm, they rounded the coastal point and saw ahead a small restaurant by a stretch of sand.

"Shall we have something to eat?" he asked.

"Yes, I am feeling hungry."

They ate on the veranda, keeping their coats on because the afternoon sun, while bright, was not very warm.

Some gravy was left on the meat dish, about three spoonfuls.

"Some more?" she asked.

"What about you?"

"I have had enough. The rest is for you."

She tipped the dish slightly, and gravy filled the large spoon. Then she poured the contents onto his plate, and returned the spoon to the dish for the next amount. Her hand was steady and sure in all its movements, and Richard again had the image of a dedicated housewife. This was, he imagined, how she would serve him if they were married.

CHAPTER EIGHT

SHE TOLD HIM THAT HER FRIENDS HAD FOUND OUT WHERE THE student was being interrogated. He was being held at a detention centre about 20 miles inland from Lisbon. She also said that one of the student leaders had been arrested and taken to the same centre.

"Does that mean," asked Richard, "that the student told them the leader's name?"

"Probably."

"Then he must have given in to torture."

"Yes, but we must not blame him too much."

"No, of course not. After all, how many of us could stand up to it?" Then a thought flashed across his mind. "But does the student leader know your name?"

Pina gazed at him for a moment before answering, "I do not know. I do not think so because I had no contact with him before the meeting, and was told about it by people who were not high in the organisation."

"Who is he?"

"He was the one who introduced the speakers." Then, "He might know my name. Yet, even if he does, he might not talk."

She looked down and up again. "But we must think about his

situation too. It is terrible. And about other people as well... if he does talk."

Two weeks passed. Then news came from Pina that the student leader had been released, along with the other student. Like the latter, he had been tortured, but had said nothing, which meant there were no subsequent arrests.

"Do you think," asked Richard, "the torture was as bad as it had been for the other student?"

"Perhaps worse, because, as a leader, he knows more."

"Yet he stood up to it."

She nodded.

For a moment, Richard found himself envying the student leader, then felt grotesque for experiencing the feeling, and managed to stifle it. He smiled, saying, "He's an example to us all."

He reflected on the suffering inflicted on the students since their decision to hold the secret meeting: one student dead, and two tortured. All three were around the same age as himself and his contemporaries at university. He tried to imagine himself, Paul and Robert in similar situations, and found it hard to. For a moment, their levels of experience seemed trivial by comparison. But, he then thought, they weren't; they were simply different, less dramatic, involving no extremes of physical pain or courage, but still valid in their own right: three complex areas among many others. Also, perhaps he, Paul and Robert, if faced with torture, might acquit themselves well; there was no way of knowing prior to the event.

Pina's eyes were rested on his face; their light suggested she could see he was thinking and was willing to let him do so undisturbed. Eventually, she said with a sigh, "And so, the life continues. The authorities will not be punished for killing or torturing, and they will do more."

"But will the students' organisation continue?"

"Oh yes. But they must now be more careful than ever. They will have to choose a new leader because the previous one will now be watched closely by the police." She smiled slightly. "All this we are used to."

CHAPTER NINE

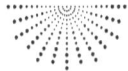

RICHARD FINISHED LATE AT THE SCHOOL. HE FELT RATHER TIRED BUT also, because he'd had a tendency to have erections throughout the day, in need of sexual stimulus. As before, he felt an impulse to go into town, drink at a few bars and look at attractive women. Though Pina remained in the back of his mind, today as every day, he desired the kind of foreground-excitement, superficial though it was, which unfortunately she could not give him.

He took the tram down the hill to the harbour area and watched the clusters of lights – signifying harbourside bars and cafes – grow nearer. Getting off the tram at a square not far from the one where he had sometimes met Pina, he walked across to a brightly lit cafe with striped awning outside it. Since the night was a little chilly, with strong breeze coming in from the harbour, he decided to go inside rather than sit at a pavement table.

There were not many customers. He brought a glass of beer and sat down. A few people were standing at the bar, a few seated at the tables. Two of the women he found attractive, but both were with men, talking and laughing, their heads close to their companions'. He finished his drink and left.

Along the road were noises coming from a cafe which didn't have tables outside, although it was also brightly lit. Richard went in and heard a crunching sound under his feet. He looked down and saw that the wooden floor was strewn with yellow peanut shells. He smiled, then noticed big jars full of peanuts on the counter – and, at both the counter and the tables, people eating peanuts and throwing the shells on the floor.

The room was crowded, especially at the bar. As Richard bought another beer, he noted that most of the people were in their twenties and thirties. He took a seat at the only empty table, in a corner by the wall, and as he drank he watched one of the waiters sweep clean a section of the floor near him. The management, he realised with a smile, did not require or expect the customers to dispose of the shells in any other way than by dropping them at their feet.

Again, he looked round the room at the people. He found several of the women quite attractive, though, as before, they all had men with them. Several of the men struck him as fairly good-looking and, in the physical sense, appropriate companions for the women. They talked a lot, gesticulating with their hands, many of which held cigarettes; and smiling broadly as the women laughed at what they said. Two of the women in particular stirred sensation in his penis, but their almost continual laughter suggested lack of depth.

He remembered the pub in London and the bar in Lisbon where he had watched groups of men play cards, seemingly perfectly at home in their surroundings. The people here also had an air of being completely at ease: so much so that, as the sound maintained a steady level and occasionally swelled, they started to become indistinguishable in his eyes. A sense of averageness returned to him, a sense of something middling and ubiquitous. For him, this something lacked poignancy, cutting edge, any capacity to capture the imagination or inspire. The reason for this, he perceived, was precisely that it was the usual, what you saw around you every day. It could not be arresting because it was not unexpected.

His mind returned to Pina and the students he had recently

been involved with. Several of these were exceptional in motivation and probably intellect, and he found it hard to imagine them mingling easily with the people he saw before him now. What, he wondered, was the essential relationship between the highly aware and committed, those who did extraordinary things and did not fit easily into crowds, and those of average level, who did fit easily?

He recalled snatches of conversation with Ray on this subject, in connection with experiences in England. He realised the question must be a universal one, applying to all societies. What, then, was the essential relation? Should the exceptionally accomplished and perceptive, in their dealings with others, pretend to be less capable and aware than they really were? Should they, in other words, play a part, for the sake of social harmony? Or should they openly display their greater ability and insight, overtly putting distance between themselves and others? And, if they did, would this breed hostility in the others, determined as the latter were to think well of themselves? So, what should the basic stance be?

The noise swelled again. Richard wryly reflected that he had come into this cafe with sex on his mind, but that had quickly been replaced by other thoughts. He glanced at his watch. It was getting late. He pushed his empty beer glass to the centre of the table and stood up.

Pina put down her coffee cup, glanced round the nearly empty café, and then opened her bag. "I want to show you what I have been reading," she said, in a hushed voice.

She brought out the book, and when he saw the word 'Marx' on the front, he recalled their previous discussion about Portuguese and British imperialism.

"It is a French book on Marx," she went on. "It was given to me by another student. One cannot buy such a book in Portugal."

She handed it to him and he leafed through the pages, remembering bits of information about Marx which he had picked up in the past.

"I think it is very important," said Pina, "for Portuguese people to read Marx. He is saying that all societies are controlled by a ruling class."

"Yes," he replied in lowered voice, "that's certainly true of Portugal, unfortunately. You have a ruling class which controls everything here and conducts colonial wars abroad."

"Of course, but what about Britain?"

"It no longer has an empire."

"But you have rich and poor?"

"Well, yes, but the difference isn't as great as in Portugal." Saying this, he recalled what she had said previously about Britain's being a generally wealthier country than Portugal partly because of the riches accrued in the past from a larger empire.

"But there is still a difference?" she asked.

After a moment, he answered, "Yes, there is." He was thinking now about the existence of public schools, to which his mother could never have afforded to send him; of restaurants and shops in the wealthy areas of London whose prices were beyond his reach; of a high life which he had seen portrayed in the cinema; and of the lives of royalty.

"I have read so," said Pina.

"Yes," he said, "and, in the past, it was much worse." He reflected on the fact that his mother's formal education had ended at the age of only 14.

"That was when your empire was at its greatest extent."

"Not my empire, or that of anyone connected with my family or friends."

"No," she smiled, "I mean the empire of your ruling class."

"Yes," seeing the point clearly for the first time, "of the ruling class."

He recollected moments from his childhood, at primary school in the early 1950s. He told Pina he remembered being shown maps of the world, with enormous areas coloured red, and being told with pride that all this had been the British Empire; also that the Empire, though now reduced, was still large. He added that he recalled wondering why, if the Empire was still so big, the school meals, for which he paid what seemed the hefty sum of sixpence, were so small: so small, in fact, that you came away still hungry. Also, he remembered several impecunious-looking teachers, who wore the same jacket all the year round, with leather covers over the elbows.

"And," Pina went on to say, "your working class was oppressed. Marx says that the working class is always exploited by the ruling class."

"And other groups are too," again thinking of the school teachers, whom, in terms of British society, he regarded as lower middle class. "Anyone who is not wealthy and powerful."

"Yes, other groups too. Marx says something about this. Where is it…" leafing through the book,

As he watched her, he found himself thinking about his recent reflections on mass-averageness; it seemed to him that, though the majority were indeed oppressed, probably in the way Marx described, many of them still remained less than inspiring. He recollected the bullies at his old school, who were all from working class backgrounds. Some members of the working class could be as obnoxious as those from any other group. And he remembered other things: as a young boy, listening on street-corners to youths in baggy, velvet-collared jackets boasting about their sexual exploits, or about fights they'd been in; watching heavily made up girls drawing deeply on cigarettes while queuing outside a local dance hall; and, on another occasion, seeing hordes of screaming girls outside a local cinema where a pop concert had just taken place; and being chased along the road with some other boys by a gang of youths, some carrying bicycle chains. He recalled other working class people as well: crowds happily packed in pubs on Saturday nights; long queues outside bingo halls; people immersed in tabloid newspapers and cheap magazines; people filling the streets like informal armies on their way to or from football matches.

Violence, tawdriness and drearily conformist behaviour were not, he knew, confined to the working class; he had, after all, had his share of jarring experiences with university students, most of whom were middle class. Also, he knew that bullying went on in public schools, to which the rich sent their children, just as much as in state schools. But the conclusion he felt was unavoidable was that one could not regard the working class as being, overall, any better than any other large social group – at least, any group not involved in exploitation. If the major problem was the existence of a ruling class, a problem almost as formidable was the very mixed quality, moral and intellectual, of the groups subordinated to that class.

"Ah, here it is," said Pina. "Marx speaks of groups who are not working class, and are exploited but think they are not."

"Yes, many different people are exploited. But how many of those would become exploiters themselves if they had the chance?"

After a moment, Pina replied, pensively, "Some perhaps."

"Some certainly."

"But not all. We must give them – how do you say – the benefit of the doubt."

"All right," he smiled, "let's give them that. No, the majority probably wouldn't become exploiters. But what *would* they become? We shouldn't assume they're all capable of unlimited development."

Then he explained to her the thoughts he'd had while she was looking through her book. As she listened, her eyelids occasionally touched together.

"Yes," she said, "I have seen similar things, at school and in the streets. I have met people of my own class, or poorer, whom I have not found interesting and not wanted as friends." She paused. "It is just that, with things so bad in this country, you put hope in everyone to try and change them, sometimes in spite of your experience. And when you read Marx, that hope is strengthened."

"But even so, you still have to come back to your experience. Yes, things are bad and of course you want to change them, but you have to be realistic about who can actually bring about change. It may not be the people, or anyway not all the people, whom Marx says it will be." He added, "I mean the working class as a whole."

"Then who?"

Again in passing, he noted the unique depth of their dialogue. Then, concentrating on her question: "People such as the best of the students."

"So, only a small number?"

"I think so."

"But if they are only small, how can they succeed?"

"I don't know. Maybe by carrying the majority along with them. But they'd still have to lead. No one else could."

Pina fell silent. As he gave her time to consider the points he had made, he reflected on what he had just said about leadership. This returned him to what he had been thinking previously, about the essential relation between the exception and the average. What if the exceptions did effectively lead the average? Would that change the basic intellectual differences between them? He could not see how it could. And would the leadership eventually run its course, with the redressing of major injustices-- leaders and led then returning to their separate intellectual and cultural milieux? Even if the leadership continued indefinitely, it looked as if intellectual and cultural division would still remain.

"I see," said Pina eventually, "that it is more complicated than I thought."

He nodded emphatically. "And than maybe Marx thought. He talks about the dictatorship of the proletariat, doesn't he?"

"Yes."

"That presumably means that the entire working class does all the inspiring, all the leading, all the originating... Something very difficult to imagine." He then expressed his doubt that effective leadership, if it ever did materialise, would be culturally unifying.

"Well, perhaps not unifying," said Pina. "But it would probably have to be permanent, because there will always be injustices to be put right."

"Yes, indeed. Can't imagine a time when they'll be no more injustices. Well, leadership may always be needed, but if leaders cannot culturally share with the led, does that mean they will be basically alone – I mean, only able to share their deepest insights with each other?"

"Perhaps it will, yes."

CHAPTER TEN

LATER, AS RICHARD THOUGHT ABOUT PINA'S LAST REPLY, A PASSAGE from Shakespeare sprang to mind: where King Henry V, on the eve of the battle of Agincourt, soliloquises on the loneliness of kingship. If he was correct in the doubts he had expressed to Pina, then things had not changed much in the intervening centuries.

When he met her next, he did not want – for the time being anyway – to continue with the subject, because of its complexity. He was slightly tense, being at a loss for what to say. However, Pina broke the silence when, with a penetrating glance, she asked, "Richard, you will be leaving Portugal soon?"

Somewhat surprised, he answered, "Yes, I suppose I will."

As he spoke, he realised he was saying this because their relationship was not sexual; if it had been, he would definitely have decided to stay.

She looked down, and he felt he knew why. In the silence that followed, he recalled previous thoughts he had had about leaving, and how, because sexual fulfilment was absent, they had tended toward the same conclusion.

Pina looked up and asked: "When does your contract finish?"

"In July."

"That is only four months."

"Yes."

She looked at him with eyes whose wide, brown steadiness was touched with intensity. "Richard, I will so miss our conversations. I have not talked with anyone as I have with you." Then, "This year has been the best of my life."

He did not know quite what to say.

"The best," she echoed.

He still said nothing, but smiled; he felt a deep satisfaction at her words, now seeing he had given her something that filled the gap left by his non-desire, something she would retain. He then had a deep sense of her capacity for gratitude, a capacity he had not seen displayed by people who had easily found sexual gratification, or who had been sexually spoilt. He thought of Paul, and his relief in finding Freda.

"For that," she said, "I want to thank you. And also for something else."

He was now slightly puzzled, and let it show in his eyes. She went on, "For giving me a feeling I never had before. For allowing me to know exactly what that feeling is like, so that I will always have the knowledge of it."

He laid his hand on hers, seeing her meaning.

"So it does not matter, Richard, that you do not love me. For me, it is enough that I love you. I have the happiness of certainty."

What she said and how she said it left him helpless to reply. His eyes lowered, and with sudden urgency he wished he could love her physically. The absence of physical desire was like a transparent but impenetrable barrier separating him from maximum intimacy with her, and for a moment he felt as if he were beating his fists against its smooth, hard surface, vainly trying to break through to the other side, where his own loneliness would end.

"Richard. I am sorry if..."

"No, it's all right, you haven't embarrassed me," raising his eyes again and smiling. "You have moved me, moved me very much, by what you have said."

"Will you," she asked, "still write to me after you have left?"

Before answering, he considered the possibility that the memory of him might stand in the way of her responding to other men, which he did not want to happen, despite a wish to maintain contact with her. He replied, "But will that be a good idea?"

The brown of her eyes clouded. "You will not write?" her voice faltering.

"I didn't say I wouldn't, but…" He then expressed his thoughts about the disadvantages of writing. "So, you see," he concluded, "I'm not being hard."

"No," after a pause, "you are not. I had not thought of it that way before."

He felt a certain sadness that he was now, inevitably, looking at their relationship from a future standpoint.

"Perhaps, Richard, we should not write, for the reason you say." Then, "I suppose I should not say this, but…"

"Go on."

"Will anyone else be interested in me in the way you have been?"

"Yes, there will be someone else," feeling that, although she would not interest many men, she would a significant few.

"I hope you are right." She smiled quickly. "But you must not worry about that. You must think of your own future."

He nodded, but knowing that his own future, like hers, would begin in loneliness. He decided to say, "Look, let's write, but you will remember what I've said?"

"I will," her eyes now steady and no longer clouded.

CHAPTER ELEVEN

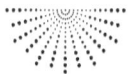

FOUR MONTHS LEFT OF HIS CONTRACT, HE PONDERED. YET SO MUCH had happened in the short time he had been in Portugal. In some ways, he realised, this had been the most eventful period of his life, just as it had been for Pina. Like her, he had known a unique intensity of relationship, and was fortified by the discoveries about his own emotions issuing from that intensity.

These discoveries pointed to permanent truths about himself; about not only how he was now, but also how he had been in the past, and how he would be in the future. His essential self, he saw, was a warm, rushing river flowing far down within him, so far down that he had only sometimes felt or heard it, because between it and his consciousness had been the rock-layers of everyday response to everyday events, and of distraction and illusion. Only now and then had he had experiences which drove down through the rock and into the rich flow, so delivering the feeling of unalloyed intimacy with self: the kind of feeling he'd had, he recalled, as a child, when the impact of basic emotional tendencies had been immediate and recurrent. Immersion in the inner river ended the limbo-state of being a stranger to yourself, of not knowing who you really were; then, the everyday self was received into the currents of the deeper self.

He now knew with absolute certainty that his deep self needed a lasting sexual relationship. Women had not played as big a part in his life as they had, for example, in Harry's, but they had played a crucial one, and he now saw that he had reacted strongly against his superficial relationships because of the need for satisfaction at a profounder level. He knew he was unable to treat sex as a game, or to juggle with relationships. He simply could not manage it, nor did he wish he could. The fact that some people were able to, he attributed to vanity.

The relatively small but significant part that women had played in his life was bound up, he felt, with his attitude toward his mother. His responsiveness to her feelings and her hardships had been symptomatic of his basic sensitivity toward women, at least to those who, in his view, deserved it. This sensitivity had been nourished by focus and concentration, not by diffuseness. Though he could not deny that this focus had been, and continued to be, blurred by lust, it always re-consolidated itself, and remained central. It was the point toward which his emotional needs always finally turned him. He knew he could have no other basic direction, that he was not free to choose any other. And the fact of his non-freedom did not bother him.

Then he considered that, like himself, other people also were not free. It looked as if Pina had not chosen the needs that were hers; nor had anyone else he knew. While it was true that some people, like perhaps Paul in deciding on a career as an accountant, evaded what they knew to be their basic needs, the fact remained that the latter existed; and, if they were not chosen, that meant they were things you discovered, not created: things you encountered but did not construct.

Suddenly, his mind turned to Daniel. He recalled Daniel's response, in their conversation in the restaurant, to what he had said about love. Daniel seemed to think that, as a homosexual, love was a possibility for him. This suggested that, beneath the showy promiscuity, there lay a need for love: again, one that was unchosen.

Richard came out of his classroom after a morning lesson and began crossing the foyer. It was Thursday, when there weren't many morning classes, and only a few people in the foyer.

A voice called out "Richard!" and he turned his head. It was Daniel, standing in the far corner, by his classroom door. Another young man was standing beside him. Richard was a little surprised at Daniel's large vocal gesture toward him.

"Do you have a moment?" asked Daniel.

Richard walked over. As he got nearer, Daniel smiled slightly, his eyes watchful, but also with a certain brightness. "Teaching going okay?" he asked.

"Yes," not expecting this question.

"Mine's more or less okay too." He swallowed, and Richard noted the movement of his large Adam's apple. Daniel's eyes turned to the man next to him, and rested on him for a moment, before he said, "This is Jão."

Looking at Jão, who smiled, Richard saw that he was about their age, with dark-brown eyes and bright teeth, "How do you do, Jão?"

"I am fine," replied Jão, with equal emphasis on each word, which suggested to Richard that he had only recently learned the expression.

"Jão's one of my best students," said Daniel, eyes now less watchful, and softer, their brightness more pronounced. Then, "We see a lot of each other outside the classroom."

Richard nodded, with an idea why Daniel had called him over, but still not completely clear.

"Excuse a moment," said Jão, and walked over to the secretary's desk.

"He's a bit behind on his lesson payments," explained Daniel. Looking now very openly at Richard, he added, "He's living with me."

"Why," Richard decided to ask, "are you telling me this?"

"Because I think I've found something deep, at last. And I wanted you to know."

"It's appreciated," with a smile.

"I hope it's going to last."

Jão returned, smiling at Daniel, then at Richard. "I have made my whole payments," he said.

CHAPTER TWELVE

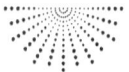

RICHARD WROTE AGAIN TO HIS MOTHER, AND TO PAUL. ONCE MORE, he reassured his mother that he was looking after himself and eating well. To Paul, he said that his contract would soon come to an end, and he was thinking about what to do next. He again did not mention Pina, because of the lengthy explanations that would subsequently require. How, he asked Paul, was the work going? As he wrote, thinking of Paul holding tightly to his relationship with Freda, his mind turned briefly to Harry. Something made him doubt that Harry was engaged yet; he didn't know if he was still in touch with Karen, and thought it likely that, since he had attended the language school on the south coast, he was teaching somewhere abroad. He was inclined to think that, if Harry was abroad, he was having a number of affairs.

Sealing the envelopes, he heard the front door open. Then there was a knock on his door. "Richard?"

"Yes, come in."

Roger appeared, smiling. "Just thought I'd let you know: Tessa and I are getting engaged."

"Congratulations."

"Well, you know how it's been with us––fast and furious. Getting engaged seemed the inevitable thing."

"Are you both planning to stay for another year?"

"Yes. It means we keep our jobs and don't run the risk of being physically separated."

"Even though," Richard added with a smile, "it means Simpson for another year? "

"You can't have everything."

Richard's smile became a grin, and he thought about the relatively easy path Roger's relationship had taken. He suggested a cup of coffee.

In the kitchen, Roger asked, "And how about you? Are you staying on?"

"No." He did not want to say anything about Pina, so he added, "One year of Simpson is enough for me."

The overcast skies and rain which had been frequent during the winter, and which had sometimes combined with strong winds coming in from the Atlantic, gradually gave way to the warmer weather of Spring. Richard welcomed the change, partly because it would make life easier in the baracas: he was mindful of what Pina had said about the difficulties caused by rain in the slums. But, he had to acknowledge, he was also relieved for more banal reasons: he could forget about his raincoat and umbrella, and could sit with more comfort at outdoor cafes.

The lessons with Pina continued, and he still saw her at weekends. They went to restaurants, the cinema, and, now that the weather was improving, returned to the coastal resorts near Lisbon. Still, they held hands or walked arm in arm.

But increasingly his mind was on the future, always the unknown quantity, which he sometimes experienced as a pressure of blankness, like the sky-pressure he had known.

He did not encounter this pressure when he and Pina talked, as they still frequently did, on a wide range of subjects, including the current political situation. Then, he felt sheltered from it, as one would from a wind by a wall. He would not, he knew, have felt it at all if sexual intimacy had been possible with her, for then the future would have offered a clear direction to follow, as it did for Roger.

Occasionally, Pina's eyes would glance intently at him from an angle, and he had an idea she was thinking of both the past and the future– her time with him and, to come, her time without him. He recalled the way she had looked at him on the train to Cescais, on their first date together.

He kept his masturbating down to once a week. In moments of intense physical desire, he found himself looking forward to returning to England and a more familiar social situation, where there would hopefully be wider opportunity to make a relationship.

Spring's sunshine strengthened into summer's, and Richard again felt the sensations of extraordinary heat he had experienced on arrival in Lisbon. The sky's blue was indigo again, and the white concrete of the buildings along the wide avenues gleamed once more. The renewed vividness of colour almost, at times, took his mind off the complexities of his relationship with Pina, and the chronic social and political problems lying behind the city's bright exteriors.

The various syllabi he had been teaching his classes were now coming to a close and the time was approaching for setting exams. Simpson gave him and the other teachers printed hand-outs as guides on how to structure the tests, but insisted that these were only to be regarded as starting-points: the teachers should always refer to the specific materials they had used in their lessons. Later, when Richard discussed this with Roger, the latter said he'd overheard the secretary tell one of the other teachers that, in previous years, students had complained that exams weren't sufficiently related to class exercises; and that, as a result, several had stopped attending.

"Which meant," said Richard, "that Simpson lost money."

"A correct deduction."

Richard began preparatory work on the tests, and, as the work grew in detail, found himself also thinking about preparations for departure. He would have to arrange his journey back, and check from his savings whether he could afford a plane or a boat. Then there would be packing to do. And talking with Roger about the flat, he had an idea that, if Roger decided to retain it, he would share it with Tessa.

Also, there would be the farewell to Pina. This was already, he felt, pre-figured in her way of saying, quietly, at the end of each lesson, "I am going now". Somehow, the phrase retained its echo even through their regular meetings at weekends, and its reverberations were reinforced when, at the end of those meetings, he would wave to her from the bus stop as she made her way alone back to her house. Perhaps the words left their indelible impression because they gently articulated resignation, accompanied as they were by a slight dilatoriness in the eyes and a lift of the eyebrows.

The tests were given, and Pina was one of the highest scorers in the class. Remembering those many moments when her grasp of English had been striking, Richard was not in the least surprised at the result. After the lesson in which he announced the marks, they had lunch together at a nearby restaurant: not his usual venue, because he did not want to share her company with the other teachers.

"Are you pleased," he asked, "about your performance?"

"Yes, very much. You are my best teacher."

"Oh, your English was already good when you started the class. Especially with all the reading you'd done. I added very little to what you already knew."

"No, you added a lot."

He smiled, recalling the time he had corrected her regarding the phrase 'a lot'. "Well, I was some help to you."

Then, "What will you do now? Go to the next stage of the course?"

Her eyelids touched together; the eye-light changed slightly. "Yes, I suppose so. With a new teacher."

Noting the change, he said, "Yes, there'll probably be a number of new people coming in September. I wonder what they'll be like."

"There will be no-one like you."

For a second, he thought of saying, 'Perhaps there will be', but decided not to. He was fairly sure – and without self-flattery – that her feeling for him would not be duplicated in the immediate future.

"I am sorry," she said.

"For what?"

"For saying how special you are to me. I did not wish to... what is the word?"

"Embarrass me?"

She nodded.

"You're not."

After a brief silence, she asked, "And what will you do next, when you go back to England?"

"Look for another teaching job, I suppose. Either in England or abroad."

"You are a very travelling man," she smiled slightly. "In Portugal, most people are not able to travel abroad because their wages are low."

"Yes, in comparison, I suppose I am privileged." He remembered her telling him that her own salary was only 2000 escudos a month, about half of his. Then another thought came to him: while the privileges, problems and complexities of having a wide range of choice were experiences unknown to most people in poor countries like Portugal, they had also been unknown to most people in Britain until after World War II. He again saw himself as a member of the educationally fortunate post-war generation In Britain. But he also reflected that that generation had not all responded to educational opportunity with equal interest, and had turned out to be, overall, a pretty mixed bag. He had a feeling that the result would be the same if educational outlets were radically increased in Portugal.

He became conscious that his mind had wandered far from Pina. His eyes, which he was now aware had drifted to the orange-coloured wall to Pina's right, returned to hers; and he saw that they were resting on his.

"It is all right, Richard. Continue thinking if you like."

He smiled at her patience. "No, I've stopped now."

"Is it something you would like to talk about?"

"Yes," deciding to recount his thoughts.

She listened, and responded, "Yes, choice is not always easy. The world is a big place, and what you say about people not all wanting education to the same extent – that would probably be true in Portugal as well."

"Probably true everywhere."

She nodded.

CHAPTER THIRTEEN

RICHARD'S FEELING OF UNCERTAINTY ABOUT THE FUTURE STARTED TO bring him back to a sense of the sky's emptiness. Even the deep blue, whose return he had welcomed, now sometimes struck him as faceless, as massively and impregnably silent. Again, he experienced a tightening in the stomach, and a limpness spreading through his body. But again he fought these sensations, clenching his fists in determination not to let them master him; and each time, after intense effort, he overcame them.

The success of these efforts was helped, in part, by keeping his mind on the day-to-day activities connected with making preparations for his departure. Classes had now finished at the school, and he spent time visiting travel offices, making enquiries, and going a last time to the P.I.D.E. headquarters, to get security clearance for his departure.

Eventually, he decided to return by ship. It would take longer but it was cheaper, and would give him a chance to view at close quarters the seas he had seen only from a high altitude on the flight out from England. He made a booking with a travel office not far from the Praca Rossio; the departure date would be July 10th.

He received a reply to his letter to his mother, and wrote back telling her of his returning date. Still awaiting a response from Paul, he decided that if he did not hear from him by July 6th, he would send a second letter.

"So, decided that one contract's enough?" asked Simpson, when Richard told him of his plans.

"I never thought I'd miss England as much as I have."

"Very patriotic," with a smile. "Of course, conditions here aren't all they might be, I fully realise. Things are a lot better back home."

Thinking of Simpson's income, Richard was tempted to reply, 'Only for some of us', but instead he agreed, "A lot better."

"All your remaining salary's been paid to you, hasn't it?"

"Yes."

"Then," holding out his hand, "it just remains for me to wish you the best of luck for your future."

With a slight smile at Simpson's sudden formality, and noting the expensive cuff-link now visible beyond his jacket sleeve, he shook the large hand that was extended to him, and found his own hold was tighter than the other's.

"So," Pina murmured, "July 10th."

He nodded, and told her about the shipping company he had booked with.

She asked, "May I come to see you off?"

Though moved by her request, he wondered – again, without self-flattery – if seeing him leave might be too stressful for her. "Are you sure you really want to?" eyes gently direct.

"I am sure. I will be all right."

Receiving no reply from Paul by July 6th, Richard wrote a second letter,

indicating his date of return. He then started to clear out his room at the flat, a job which turned out to take much longer than he had expected. When it was completed, all that remained was packing. Because of books and other things he had bought in Lisbon, he found he would need an extra suitcase, and discovered a shop near the school which sold luggage at cheaper prices than in the centre of town.

Everything was ready. On the 9th, he phoned Pina to arrange to meet. As he put the coins in the slot, and heard the click at the other end when the receiver was picked up, he was reminded of the first time he had ever phoned her. Her voice, soft as always, travelled along the wires: "Si?"

He told her the time of the ship's departure, and suggested a meeting point near the port entrance.

"I will be there, Richard."

The morning was very bright, but not excessively hot. Richard stood on the flat's balcony and felt the strong breeze blowing across the city from the harbour. Behind him, he heard Roger's voice: "All set, then?"

Turning round, he smiled and nodded, glancing at his suitcases that stood, sealed and labelled, in the middle of the lounge floor.

Roger went on, "We haven't had much of a chance to chat just recently, I know. Things seem to have happened so quickly."

"Yes, they have."

"Anyway, I've been wanting to tell you that you've been a damned good flatmate."

"Well, thanks."

"It's because you don't impose."

"You don't either."

" Well, I've learned that from you."

Richard noted that Roger was, in this respect at least, self-critical. While he had not displayed a searching mind, he was now showing he had recognised an area in which he had needed to improve.

"By the way," said Richard, changing the subject, "will you be staying on in the flat?"

"Yes, Tessa's moving in."

Richard nodded, recalling his prediction to this effect. "Well, I hope everything goes the way you want it to." Then, "Will you say goodbye for me to the other teachers?"

"Sure."

"And could you wish Daniel good luck for me? He'll know what's meant."

"Sure," with a smile.

"Thanks."

They exchanged English addresses. Then the taxi arrived. Roger held out his hand: "Safe journey back."

"Thanks again. And safe stay in Portugal."

From the balcony, Roger waved as the taxi engine started. Then the taxi turned the corner of the street, into the shadows of the downward-sloping side road that led in the general direction of the harbour.

As the vehicle slowed along the road which skirted the harbour, Richard saw Pina in the distance, waiting at the arranged spot, the main entrance gate. Through the bars of the barrier that extended to the gate, he could see his ship.

Pina's figure drew nearer. He did not now, as he had before, feel an impulse to imaginarily convert it to one more physically attractive, and was slightly ashamed that he had ever wanted to. It seemed an attempt to violate the wholeness of her identity, to pick and choose between different parts of her self-hood, when what he should have done was to accept all the parts, since they were inextricably linked.

He could now make out the colour of her shoes. Her face turned in his direction; she must have just heard the sound of the car. He signalled to the driver, and the vehicle slowed to a halt. Through the window, he saw her see him, and her face widen into a smile, though her eyes had a slightly strained look. He smiled too, and opened the door.

"Richard! I was a little worried because I was not sure I had come to the right place."

"Yes, this is the place." He paused before adding, "That is my ship, over there."

She looked in the direction of the vessel, then back at him; her smile contracted. "And it leaves in three quarters of an hour?"

He nodded. Then he glanced at the driver, and saw he was impatient to be paid. He gave him the fare plus a tip, and the driver got his luggage out. The taxi pulled away.

"Well," he said to Pina, "we'll have to carry the luggage to the ship." He asked her to take the small suitcase while he picked up the two large ones. As they walked along, he realised he had under-estimated the weight of the cases, and was feeling pressure on his thighs and groin. Under the bright sun, his forehead began to moisten. The quay was about two hundred yards away.

"Ol! Ol!" he heard to his left. A porter was driving toward him on a mobile luggage-carrier. At the welcome sight, he dropped his cases and waited for the porter to stop.

"We're rescued," he smiled to Pina. There were some beads of sweat on her cheek; dropping her case, she smiled a little.

They put their things onto the carrier and, because there was enough empty space left, the porter gesticulated for them to get on too. At this, Pina's smile widened slightly. Richard held her arm as the carrier gathered some speed, making its way toward the gangplank that was placed diagonally against the ship's side. In front of the plank was a long table with two men in uniform standing behind it. People were queuing at the table and Richard assumed that this was where passports were being checked. To the right of the table, about twenty feet along, he saw an opening in the ship's side, where baggage was being stowed.

The carrier stopped. Richard thanked the driver and gave him two escudos.

"Well, did you enjoy your ride?" he asked Pina.

"Yes, it was unexpected," maintaining her smile.

"Come on, let's join the queue by the table."

As they did so, he took her hand and pressed it, sensing she was doing her best to fight sadness. At the gesture, her eyes looked up into his; their previously strained look had been replaced by what he now recognised as the mild light of acceptance. Her smile, though not widening further, was settled. She said, "Richard, I am all right… as I said I would be."

The man in uniform returned Richard's passport to him with a nod, and he and Pina went toward the baggage-hold.

Two of the ship's sailors offered to help them with their things, and, at the hold, lifted them to the man inside.

A hooting sound came from one of the ship's funnels. Richard looked at his watch and saw there were only 25 minutes left before departure. He told Pina they would have to join the queue by the gangplank.

She nodded. Then, "Oh, I have not given you my address," putting her fingertips to her lips.

"That's right. All I know is the number of your house. I never bothered to check the street name. And I haven't given you my address either – I completely forgot."

Rummaging in his pocket for a piece of paper, he found one that was creased with some pocket fluff on it. He asked Pina to write on the top part, then entered his details on the bottom half, tore it off and gave it to her. The hurry and improvisation made him feel awkward and uneasy: the effort seemed inappropriately makeshift for a moment such as this. His unease was sharpened when he saw, behind him, a middle-aged couple nod their heads to indicate that he should keep moving forward with the queue.

Ahead, people had started mounting the gangplank, which creaked slightly under their weight. At the foot of the plank, an official was checking people's tickets, and Richard realised that Pina would not be able to accompany him onto the ship. He turned to her.

"Yes," she said, "this is where I must stay." She looked at him intently, and he heard a breath escape her; but still her smile remained.

The official was now just three people away.

"Richard, I will always…" and she stopped. Then, "I want you to be very happy."

"And I want you to be."

Her lips were touching his cheek; her eyes were closed. Then her face lowered.

"Bilhiet-os!" called the official. "Bilhietos, obrigado!"

Richard produced his ticket, and the man fixed his eyes on it for a moment before nodding. Richard looked again at Pina, whose eyes were now lifted to his; they had once again become mild, seeming wider than ever. He squeezed her hand, and she his.

Then he mounted the gangplank. Its creaking sound recurred. At the top, he immediately sought an opening by the deck rails, finding one about 10 yards along. From here, he could see Pina looking up, in an unfocussed way, at the top of the gangplank. He called out to her three times, loudly, because other passengers were also calling to people below. Her head did not move, and he realised she had not heard him. Then her head turned to the side of the gangplank opposite him. He was sure that, when she had failed to spot him there, she would look on his side. After about a minute, her head did turn his way, and he began waving his arm vigorously.

She saw him. Her left hand went to the corner of her eye. With the other, she waved back in slow movements. She did not call out – perhaps, Richard thought, because she knew she would be inaudible, or because she did not feel able to. His waving now slowed, to keep time with hers.

The gangplank was being wheeled back. Richard felt the deck-rail press slightly, momentarily, into his stomach, and Pina's face, along with all the others on the quayside, became a little smaller. Shiny wavelets now lapped against the bottom of the ship. Pina's face was still distinguishable, and he could see that her left hand had lowered from it. But within a minute it was a featureless roundness. Then he could not see her at all, only a mass of heads. The water between the ship and the quay was becoming bluer. From a sudden sense of unbridgeable separation, he gripped the deck rail.

His eyes rested on a silent crowd surrounded by asphalt flatness, behind which the movement of cars was visible. Still holding the deck-rail, he reflected on Pina's words, "I will always", and felt he knew what she meant. He lowered his head, pondering the decisiveness, for them both, of the year that had just passed.

CHAPTER FOURTEEN

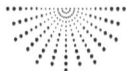

THE SEA WAS DEEP-TROUGHED, WITH PATCHES HARSHLY BRILLIANT from the afternoon sun. Land was out of sight. The conversation around him had ceased to be a vague hum, and voices were now distinct and varied. There were a number of English people, and some Americans; also, French and Spanish, and a few Portuguese. They were mainly then, Richard concluded, tourists who had been holidaying in Portugal. To his left, he heard a portable radio playing pop music: a sound, he now realised, he'd rarely heard for a whole year. He found himself relating pop music to the kind of social conditions – for example, in Britain or America – which were much more certain and secure than those in Portugal; and it was to these kinds of conditions that he was now returning.

How, he wondered, would he be re-assimilated into them? What would he do next? But no sooner had he asked the questions than he wanted to be relieved of the weight of them, and he began mingling with the crowd, along the decks and down the narrow stairways between decks. On the middle deck, he came to the ship's bar, and bought a bottle of strong-tasting lager.

When he went out onto the open deck again, the sun had lowered, and its light was milder on the water-surface. He calculated that the ship would soon be entering the Bay of Biscay, and that the night would be spent crossing it. They should be arriving in Portsmouth about noon the following day.

His thoughts drifted back to Pina. He was sure she would write to him, but now he wasn't sure if he would reply. As he had thought before, perhaps it was best if she put him behind her, and maybe the way to ensure this was not to answer her letters. On the other hand, not replying would hurt her. He was uncertain about what to do.

Evening was approaching; the sun was an orange ball which could be gazed at without squinting, hovering just above the sea-line. He knew that the ship was still too far south for the sunset to be extended, and was reminded of Lisbon's quick descents into darkness after the sun had dropped below the horizon.

He was now feeling chilly, and returned to the covered area. He had a meal in the ship's cafeteria, then set about finding a comfortable seat for the night. In the lounge, he spotted one and went over. His watch said 7 pm. Though it was still early, he thought he should now stay put. As the evening wore on, he watched the other seats steadily fill up.

Sometime after the lights were dimmed at about 10 pm, he started to feel the rocking of the boat more distinctly, and guessed this was due to the winds for which the Bay of Biscay was renowned. For a while, the movement kept him awake, and he experienced a slight queasiness in the stomach. But eventually, with his eyes closed, came the gradual slackening of consciousness which he knew as the path to sleep.

His eyes opened to early morning light. Around him, people lay at different angles asleep in their seats. He got up and made his way as quietly as he could to the toilet area; there, after urinating, he washed his hands, using the soap and paper towels which he found provided. When he returned to his seat, he noted that a few other people were now awake. He picked up his small hold-all containing his razor and toothbrush and went back to the toilet area, to get a sink before queues started. In walking about, he realised the boat was much steadier than it had been the night before.

He was one of the first to arrive at the cafeteria for breakfast. He bought coffee and buttered rolls and sat at a corner table. Then he went out onto the deck.

The sea was now more green than blue: almost the colour, he recalled, of the water on the south coast resorts he used to visit as a child. He guessed that they were now near northern France.

The sky had a wide cloud-bank just above the sea-line, and a strong breeze was blowing across the warmth shed by the sun, which stood at the top edge of the cloud. Richard leant out from the deck rail, letting the breeze blow his hair back, and enjoyed the winnowing feel of it from his forehead to his hair-crown.

A little later, he heard someone say in English that he'd been told that the ship was behind schedule because of the winds during the night, and would not be arriving in Portsmouth till mid-afternoon. 'So I'll be in London,' thought Richard, 'by mid-evening.' He wondered what expression his mother would have when she opened the door and saw him.

Toward noon, cloud began to accumulate far above the sea-line and covered most of the sky, leaving room for only sporadic bursts of sunshine. But it later diminished, and by about 1 pm the sun stood unchallenged, with clear blue all around it. The heat was not as strong as in Portugal, but it was still considerable.

Richard went down to the cafeteria for lunch, and when he came up again, he was able to make out a thin, horizontal line, just darker than the sea's. He smiled, knowing immediately it was the south coast of England. Once more, he leant out, for the wind to blow his hair back.

The line slowly thickened and became green. Soon, he could distinguish between a green background and white-and-grey foregrounds which he knew to be built-up areas. An announcement came over the tannoy that they would be arriving in Portsmouth in about an hour.

As the boat moved slowly past the high, white sides of naval ships at anchor, Richard joined in the queue of passengers forming on the upper deck. Between two battleships, the quayside came into view, clustered with people.

Going down the gangplank, Richard saw the quayside crowd rushing forward and greeting passengers; and he heard more people speaking English at the same time than he had for a year. Again he smiled, now joining a second queue to collect his baggage.

Once through customs, he was helped by a porter to carry his things to a nearby taxi rank, where he asked to be taken to the station.

CHAPTER FIFTEEN

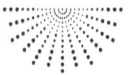

AT THE STATION, A PORTER'S HELP WAS AGAIN REQUIRED, TO STOW HIS bags in the luggage van of the London train, which was due to depart only fifteen minutes after his arrival.

As the train left the town's suburbs, Richard saw at close quarters the green of fields and hills which had been previously been visible to him at sea. This kind of green – thick and deep – he had not seen for a whole year, and he contrasted it with the brighter but sparser variety he had known in Portugal.

For the second day in succession, he watched the sun set, but now knew its after-light would stay in the sky, adding to the warmth of a July evening.

London neared. Soon, Richard could make out the dome of St Paul's Cathedral, and other landmarks on the tawny-tinged horizon. As his eye moved across the grey-and-orange of the city, from nearby houses to middle distance to skyline, he was impressed as never before by the largeness of the city. Lisbon could be placed in just one of the areas his gaze scanned. But immediately he thought of the depth of his experience in that smallish city, and from this standpoint its size did not matter.

The train was going more slowly now, and the number of rail-lines had increased. Eventually, the shadow of Paddington Station fell over his carriage, and he looked up at the steel girders networked beneath the roof. The train, despite its slowness, jolted as it stopped.

Coming out onto the platform, Richard was struck by the brightness of the station lights. This, as much as the panorama he had viewed from the train, gave him a vivid sense of being back in London.

From the window of his taxi, he could see that the traffic was heavy, and he was reminded that this was the later part of the rush hour. As the vehicle crawled along, he settled back in his seat, knowing he was in for a slow ride at least until they were away from the city centre.

He began thinking about his mother. She knew, from his letters, that he would be arriving today, but of course she did not know – as he hadn't – at what time exactly. He reflected that she must have missed him a lot.

The driver helped him with his cases down the stone steps to his door. Breathing quite hard, he paid and tipped him. Alone again, he paused before putting his index finger to the doorbell.

The door, partly brightened by light from the lamp-post nearby, opened slowly. His mother's small face appeared at the side of it, her eyes shoving uncertainty,

"Hello, Mum. I'm back."

Her eyes filled with light and her face broke into a smile. "Richard! Oh, Richard!" putting her arms around his neck. "You've come home safely."

"Yes," he smiled, kissing her forehead. "Safe and sound."

"You must be starving," she said, as he came into the hallway.

He smiled, noting that this had been the next thought to come into her head. "Yes. I am hungry," putting his cases by the hall-stand.

In the living room, he saw that table had been set.

"I didn't know what time you were arriving so I didn't know when to start cooking."

Despite his long absences in recent years, her words retained a familiar ring.

"I'll put everything on now," she quickly added.

Over the meal, he talked about Portugal, adding to what he had already told her in his letters. But he did not mention Pina, or the political troubles. As she listened, her eyes sometimes rounded in appreciation of new, unknown things. A couple of times, her eyes took in the whole of his face and she smiled, as if not quite listening to what he was specifically saying; it was a gesture he knew well.

His bed was made with spotless, freshly-ironed sheets. He smiled, not having slept in such a bed for a long time. He was by now quite tired, feeling the effects of having spent the previous night in a chair. Soon after laying his head on the pillow, he began to drift toward sleep.

Waking to the early morning light, he found himself thinking about Paul, and wondering why he hadn't answered his penultimate letter. He recalled the comparison he had drawn between Paul and Pina, in respect of their gratitude at finding deep companionship with a member of the opposite sex.

After breakfast, he took a walk down the road to the small group of shops which he could remember from childhood. Looking into the shop windows, and wandering through the surrounding streets, he again had that feeling of being alienated from them which he had first experienced during university vacations. This sense of distance persisted when he went into the confectioner's and recognised one of the staff who had been there when he was a boy, and who had aged considerably. When he bought a bar of chocolate, she took his money without any recognition in her eyes.

On the way home, he realised that his sense of detachment was now connected with uncertainty about the future. He had no anchorage, not knowing what direction to take next. He was relieved, when he got home, to hear his mother tell him what she was making for lunch; this turned his mind to simpler things.

That night, he masturbated, thinking of Jill. Afterwards, his thoughts went to Pina; he imagined her alone in bed, in the darkness, like himself. Perhaps she had recently masturbated over him. What would the future hold for her?

Several days passed, without a letter from Paul. Richard began to think that maybe Paul was no longer living with his parents and that they were, for some reason, not passing letters on to him. But then, at the start of the following week, an envelope with Paul's handwriting on it lay on the doormat.

Paul apologised for his delay in replying, but said he had been going through a difficult period recently. He would tell him more about this when they met, and suggested a get-together at a pub in Ilford the following Saturday. He gave travel directions. Richard wrote back confirming the arrangement.

He over-estimated the time it would take him to get to the pub, and arrived early. His eyes scanned the bar area and he saw that Paul had not come yet. Buying a glass of beer, he wondered what Paul would be telling him this evening. He took a seat at an empty corner table and waited.

Three men came in together; then there was a gap. A young couple appeared, and just behind them Richard could see a fair-haired man wearing glasses. Paul. As the couple moved off to the left. Richard raised his arm for Paul to see him. Paul's face registered recognition. He smiled slightly and walked toward him with his customary short steps. Richard stood up, smiling too, and held out his hand.

"Hello, Paul."

"Hello."

"It's been some time," as their hands met. "What will you have?"

"Oh, just a half of cider."

Reminded of Paul's modest capacity for alcohol, Richard walked over to the bar and got his drink. As he handed it to him, he noticed that his eyes, behind the glass lenses, were curiously lit: they seemed to express both curiosity and uncertainty. He sat down, not quite sure of what to say next.

"I was very interested," said Paul, "by what you said in your letters. It must be quite an experience –actually working in another country. I've only ever been abroad on holiday."

"Yes, it was an eye-opener in many ways," Still noting the play of light in Paul's eyes, he began to say more about the experiences which had gone into his letters: the slums and poverty, the political regime. Also, he now told him about the incident on the university campus.

"That," said Paul. "is what I call things happening to you."

"Yes, there was plenty going on,"

"Makes me feel like a stay-at-home."

"I didn't," Richard came in quickly, "tell you these things so that you'd start criticising yourself."

"I know," looking down and then up again. "Please carry on. I imagine there's even more to tell."

Richard hesitated. Should he mention Pina? He decided he would. Speaking fairly slowly, and recalling the way he had talked about it to Roger, he briefly described the complex situation.

Paul listened attentively and in silence. His eyes showed, not curiosity, but sympathy: the quality that was now counterbalanced with uncertainty.

"Yes," he said, when Richard had finished speaking, "I see that just being with her was so vital to you."

Richard nodded, sensing that Paul was thinking of the parallel with his relationship to Freda.

"Though," Paul went on, "it wasn't a matter of sex not being very important, because there was no sex at all."

"That's right."

Paul seemed to muse, eyes on his beer glass. "It's certainly an extraordinary thing."

Richard silently appreciated this last comment.

Paul looked at him again. "But you decided not to continue the relationship?"

"It wouldn't have been fair to her. The longer it would have gone on, the stronger she'd have felt for me."

Paul nodded; the sympathetic light in his eyes had strengthened. "Let me get you another drink."

"Okay."

When Paul returned from the bar, the uncertainty in his eyes was less distinct. "I was," he said, "intending to spend a fair bit of time tonight talking about the complications in my life. I stupidly assumed I was the only one who'd had difficulties."

"Well," not minding changing the subject, "let's talk about yours."

"Okay. They're nothing to do with Freda, though."

"Then with your job?"

Paul paused before replying, "Is it that obvious?"

"Not obvious, no. I just had a hunch."

Paul smiled a little. "The job, yes. You were right when you said it wouldn't give me intellectual satisfaction."

Richard decided just to nod.

Paul want on, "The problem is, I don't know if there's anything else I can change to."

Richard recalled Paul's previous indications that he lacked confidence about performing in public view.

Paul's head began turning slowly from side to side, in a way Richard had seen before. "I want to keep a low profile – for fear, as I've said, of my limitations showing. But I also want to have a go at something that's going to stretch me intellectually. Because I don't want to end up in the kind of situation Matthew Arnold describes. You know – being in 'a brazen prison' – tied to 'some unmeaning taskwork'. Those lines made an impact on me when I first read them at university, and the impact's stuck."

Appreciating what Paul was saying, Richard waited a moment before replying, "Stretching yourself intellectually would mean taking chances. I thought you said you didn't want anything chancy."

"I didn't, before."

"Taking chances," Richard continued, deciding to express all his thoughts on the subject, "entails the risk of failure."

"I know. I don't mind failing in private, where others can't see me."

"But if you're doing a job, someone's going to see you, obviously."

"Yes," exhaling.

Richard immediately added, "I'm not saying this to discourage you."

"But to make me think realistically."

"Yes. Because I also know how complex the problem is. We all want a job that brings out our deepest capacities, and confirms our identity as individuals. A job which is real self-discovery, self-encounter. Like the experience of love and friendship."

"I take it," said Paul, "that you've not yet found that kind of job either."

"No," realising his words had revealed more than he had intended. "I'm far from sure about continuing the kind of teaching I've been doing."

"Finding the right kind of job," Paul continued, "ends a sort of loneliness. Just as finding love and friendship ends another sort."

"Yes. We all want all kinds of loneliness to end."

"And I suppose that at least , even if you fail in doing something that puts you in touch with yourself, it's less difficult to bear than failure in doing something that doesn't."

"Even with witnesses."

Paul nodded.

"So," Richard asked, "what's it going to be?"

"Well. I've got to think more about it, of course. But I'll be looking for something meaningful."

"The same applies to me."

Richard picked up his drink. So did Paul. The silence that followed felt natural and inevitable to Richard, and he did not try to think of other things to say. Paul looked more relaxed than previously; the uncertainty had gone from his eyes – replaced, not exactly by certainty, but by a steady pensiveness which did not appear to cause discomfort.

Paul eventually broke the silence with "I should have said this earlier, but I'm really glad you're back."

Richard did not quite know how to reply.

"One more?" asked Paul, pointing to his glass, as if to save him the trouble of thinking of something to say.

"But it's my round."

"Oh, that doesn't matter."

"One more, then."

Paul said he would be in touch again soon, and Richard waved to him from the bus platform as his figure got smaller in the semi-darkness of the side road. When he took a seat, he felt satisfaction at tonight's renewal of openness.

CHAPTER SIXTEEN

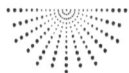

RICHARD'S THOUGHTS TURNED TO RAY. RAY HAD NOT REPLIED TO THE letter he had written him before leaving for Portugal. He knew this wasn't because Ray could not contact him, since he had asked him to reply to his London address so that letters could be forwarded to Portugal. What, then, was the reason? Perhaps Ray was living a very full life in Manchester, had made lots of friends, or had married. Perhaps even, he had changed in outlook. Anyway, after a year, it didn't look as if he was going to continue with the relationship: one which Richard had prized, and which Ray too had seemed to value highly.

He decided that, because of the amount of time that Ray had let elapse, he would not write to him. Ray may well have had good reasons for not wanting to maintain a regular correspondence, but he should have at least let Richard know about them. The absence of such a gesture now made communication on his part seem inappropriate.

In connection with the apparent demise of his relationship with Ray, he thought also about the ending of his period at university, and meditated on how an important phase of one's life could come to a close either suddenly or within a short time, leaving no follow-through. He now found it difficult to see his life as a clearly defined continuum: as it had appeared to be when he was studying for school exams, and when the day-to-day pattern of living had been simpler. Would it go on being difficult to connect the present with the past?

He began re-considering what to do next professionally. In his doubtfulness, he sometimes felt as if his feet were off the ground and he was moving through a kind of ether which no sound penetrated. The ether was transparent, so that he could see things in the distance, but those things were beyond the ether, while he remained within it.

The sensation put him in mind of the sky-feeling. Though not the same as it, it had the same effect of placing him in silent isolation, one which he had to find a way out of, unaided. The only way out, he realised, was through concentrated thinking on action.

Yet even action, he sensed, was not a route to absolute certainty, or to any place where you could be permanently sure of your bearings. He was immediately reminded of past thoughts on this subject. Action was a pressing forward, forward and onward, toward you did not know exactly what. No matter how definite or effective the action was, it always filled only one bit of space at a time, with emptiness always lying ahead of it.

No, action wasn't a route to certainty, but it was still called for. The space it occupied was small, but still that space had to be covered. He thought not just about job-directions but also about the literary ambitions he had once discussed with Ray: the aim of researching into what made the physical world tick, and of writing a book or books to convey his findings. Briefly, he meditated on his atheistic position, and was convinced that this would be central to his thinking from now on, always sounding as the bass note.

He also thought about the church near his home, the one which he had previously considered to be somehow connected with the answer to his question about the basic dynamics of the physical world. As an atheist, he did not regard religion as providing that answer; yet perhaps, by understanding why religion had come about, he could get closer to the solution.

CHAPTER SEVENTEEN

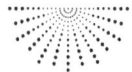

HE HELD THESE DIFFERENT AREAS OF THINKING SIMULTANEOUSLY IN HIS mind as he began scanning the papers for job advertisements. He bought various dailies, but also started reading the weekly Times Educational Supplement. Again, the question loomed: should he go on teaching, and, if so, should it be of the same kind?

One morning, a pale yellow envelope appeared on the doormat, with a cluster of stamps at one corner. 'Pina,' he thought immediately. When he picked the envelope up, he recognised her large script, and recalled how she would hold a pen when writing in class. He swallowed.

She began the letter by saying she had enrolled for the next stage of the English course, and that she was finding it interesting. She also told him how her job was going, and that there was talk at the university of renewed political activity.

In the final paragraph, occupying the last few lines, she said she hoped he wouldn't mind if she told him she missed him. After that came the phrase "Very much," and another full stop. Then, she would be "very happy" if he replied and told her what he was doing.

A bending of his fingers folded the letter in half. He remembered his agreement with her that they would write, but also his later misgivings about it. He sensed from her wording – and it came as no surprise – that there was no-one else in her life, that he was still the focus of her emotions. Should he reply, or not? As he put the letter in his pocket, he had the disconcerting realisation that he now possessed the same power which Ray, for whatever reason, had apparently exercised: that of terminating a relationship which the other person clearly wanted to continue.

His job search continued. He saw an advertisement for a post of teacher of English as a Foreign Language at an institute called the British School in Milan, Italy, starting in September. As with the job in Portugal, teaching would be by direct method, so no prior knowledge of Italian was required. Application was by letter and curriculum vitae. Though still not certain whether he wished to continue language teaching, he decided to try for it since it was only a one year contract.

About a week after he had posted the application, an envelope arrived with an Italian postmark. He opened it and read that he was being offered the post. If he wished to accept it, could he please reply immediately, and arrange to be in Milan by September 15th? The school would refund his travel costs on arrival.

Should he say 'yes'? His uncertainty persisted, but mingled now with pleasure and gratitude at having received the offer, and with re-assurance at such a positive result to this, his first job application since Portugal. After two days' deliberation, he wrote and posted a letter of acceptance.

When he told his mother of his decision, she smiled quickly, saying "Oh, marvellous," but also lowered her eyes, a gesture which indicated to him that she would have liked him to stay on at home, at least for a while longer.

He rang Paul.

"Oh, well that's quick," said Paul. "Congratulations."

"Yes, I didn't think I'd have an offer on my first application."

"We'll have to get together before you go. Shall I come down your end?"

"Okay."

They arranged to meet at the tube station near his home, and to go along to a nearby pub. On the way there, Richard wondered what further thoughts, if any, Paul had had about changing his job.

"Paul!" he called, as he saw him appear at the top of the escalator and hand his ticket to the collector. Paul looked in his direction, smiling slightly. Then he walked toward him, holding out his hand. "Congratulations, once again."

"Don't congratulate me too soon. I don't know what the job's going to be like."

"Well, at least you're trying something out. And going abroad again."

"Yes," remembering how Paul had previously described himself as a stay-at-home. "Anyway, let's go and have a drink."

Putting down Paul's glass of cider, Richard asked, "So, what about your trying something out?"

"Yes, indeed. I've thought of maybe charity administration."

"Would that stretch you intellectually?"

"Yes, in the sense that I'd have to make decisions, weigh up possibilities."

"Decisions affecting other people?"

Paul nodded. Then, "It's the sort of thing I'd like to take on." He drank some of his cider. "And if it doesn't work out, then it doesn't."

'That's more like it,' Richard nearly said. Smiling, he asked, "Have you discussed this with Freda?"

"Yes. She says if I want to go ahead, I should."

"I second that."

After a moment, Paul went on: "I'm beginning to see that it's important to have pluck. You can't side-step your way through life."

Richard nodded in reply.

They discussed ways in which Paul might find work in this new field. Richard mentioned certain newspapers and journals which he knew ran advertisements for charities.

Eventually, they returned to the subject of Richard's new job. Richard told Paul he had to be in Milan by September 15th. Immediately Paul said that this was "very soon", then asked, "Do you plan to keep in touch with Pina?"

Richard paused before replying "I don't know," and briefly explained the doubts he'd had about maintaining contact by letter.

"I see," said Paul.

Richard, not wanting to say any more about Pina, asked Paul how Freda had done in her final examinations.

"Oh, very well. She got a 2I." Then, "We try to see each other as much as we can. About one weekend in three." I think I'll soon be popping the question to her."

"Marriage?"

"I'd say it's time," the light in his eye suggesting someone who has reached a place of rest.

"The best of luck."

When they parted, Richard said he would be in touch before leaving, then wished Paul success in his job search. Paul held out his hand.

CHAPTER EIGHTEEN

AFTER MUCH THOUGHT, RICHARD DECIDED NOT TO RESPOND TO PINA. He felt it would be best for her in the long run. He repressed the tendency to try and imagine her facial expression at the absence of a reply letter.

Turning his thoughts to Italy, he opted for travelling by train rather than plane; he had, after all, time to spare, and wanted to use the opportunity to see more of the Continent. He checked on the fare and found that he would easily be able to afford a sleeper's compartment. He booked for departure on September 12th, to allow himself enough time to find temporary accommodation in Milan before reporting for work on the 15th.

Also, he bought himself a *Teach Yourself Italian* book and learned some basic expressions.

"Hello?" said Paul, at the other end of the receiver.

"Paul, it's Richard. Just ringing to say that I'll be leaving for Italy the day after tomorrow."

"The day after tomorrow?"

"Yes. Sorry I haven't phoned you sooner, but I've been busy with final preparations."

"Oh, right." Then, "But there won't be time for us to meet before you go."

"Why not?"

"Well, tomorrow night's the only time I could have made, and I'm afraid I'm tied up."

"I see."

"But you'll send me your new address?"

"As soon as I get it."

After a brief silence, Paul said, "So, once more you head off into the horizon."

"You make it sound more adventurous than it really is."

"It's pretty adventurous." Then, "Be in touch."

"Now, darling, are you sure you've got everything?"

"Yes I'm sure."

His mother handed him a small pack wrapped in greaseproof paper. "Some sandwiches for you. I thought you might get peckish on the train."

"Thanks."

"You'll write as soon as you can?"

"Of course."

He kissed her forehead. From the door, she waved. Making his way to the bus-stop, he increasingly felt the weight of his cases. In the bus, there was just enough room to stow the luggage, because the rack already had some bags in it.

The station was crowded, and echoed with the sound of a voice giving information over the tannoy system: the kind of sound, he reflected, with which he was now quite familiar.

He checked the number on his ticket and found his carriage. He assumed the same number would apply to his compartment in the link-up train at Calais, the one with the sleeper. Once settled in his seat, he ate his sandwiches.

It was late afternoon when his train pulled into Dover.

The sight of the white cliffs reminded him of his holiday with Ray, and of the thoughts he had had about World War II in connection with Dover. Briefly, he meditated again on Ray's failure to write.

The ferry crossing was smooth. From the upper deck, Richard once again watched the sun lower toward the sea-line.

At Calais, the link-up train was longer and wider than the London-Dover one. With his ticket number now firmly in his memory, he moved along the train corridor, and finally found his carriage: it had a made-up bunk in its top right-hand corner. Outside, it was getting dark and he switched on the compartment light.

Across the window sped occasional points of light: farmhouses, cars. He knew the train was travelling south-east and wondered where exactly they were now. Eventually, he felt his eyelids lowering. He went and brushed his teeth in the small wash-room along the corridor and, on returning, locked the carriage door behind him. Climbing up into his bunk, he found it softer than he had expected. As he pulled the bed sheets over him, he wondered if he would be able to sleep against the sound of the train. Soon, he felt the loosening of consciousness which told him he would.

He awoke to early daylight, with a dry taste in his mouth. The shuttling movement of the train returned to his ears. Under the bedclothes, he felt warm but knew he would have to get up and drink something. He unlocked his case and took out a bottle of mineral water he had bought at Calais station. The water was sharply cold against his throat, and a few mouthfuls dispelled the thirst.

Through the window, he could see undulating landscape: green – though, as in Portugal, not quite as green as England. The land was dotted with tree copses, and on the horizon was the sheen of a river.

After washing and shaving in the wash-room, he returned to his compartment and sat down for a while, looking out of the window; though he wanted to have some breakfast, he knew they would not yet be serving it.

He waited about half an hour, and then made his way along the corridor, past a number of compartments, to the dining car. There, he ordered coffee, with rolls, butter and jam. He asked the waiter which part of the country they were now in.

"Pres du Loire. Et puis, les montagnes."

So, near the Loire: hence the sheen on the horizon; and later, they would be going into the mountains. The dining car was filling up and Richard, rather than return to the solitude of his compartment, decided to stay there. Around him, people were talking: mostly in French, but he also heard snatches of Italian and German. There were several young couples, and families with children of different ages, plus several elderly people. Many talked animatedly, giving him the impression that they knew exactly where they stood with each other, and what direction their lives were going in.

He realised that this impression was probably an exaggeration of the truth, but it set him thinking about himself. He felt he would give the impression, to anyone who noted his presence, of not knowing exactly where he was headed; and that impression would be correct. Once more, he thought of what Ray had said about always moving forward into new kinds of uncertain situations. Uncertainty was fundamental to any searching mind, so there was nothing wrong in feeling it. Making a decision about going to work in another country, about effecting any major change in your life, was based always on partial information, partial clarity. Any claim to total knowledge was fatuous.

The morning passed. Not wanting lunch, Richard returned to his carriage and read for a while. Mid-day moved into afternoon. The sheen on the horizon had long ago disappeared, and now Richard saw the dark blue of mountains, well above the land-line, their summits white. The Alps, he knew. Slowly, the mountains got higher, and the train was moving on an upward gradient, its engine audibly tugging against the pressure of the slope. The lowering sun disappeared from view prematurely behind indigo walls, and shadows were thrown across the carriage. Richard put the light on. It was now impossible to see the tops of the mountains. Richard realised that the night would be spent passing beneath them, and he wondered if, by morning, the train would be on flat land again.

He returned to the dining car for the evening meal, and practised his French by talking a little more to the waiter he had spoken to that morning. Later, back in his carriage, he continued reading, then decided to have an early night.

CHAPTER NINETEEN

ON WAKING, RICHARD HEARD THE TRAIN ENGINE CHUGGING FAST AND freely, and knew they were out of the mountains. Through the window was undulating green, with the train on a downhill gradient. Dotted across the green were farmhouses.

The air was noticeably warmer than on the previous day, and Richard felt more relaxed as he washed and shaved.

Returning to his carriage, he heard the train slowing down; through the window, he could see that they were not at a station. Then a voice echoed along the corridors: "Passeporte! Passeporte!" They were now, then, at the Italian border. He handed his black booklet to the sturdily-built guard who appeared at his doorway. The man flipped through its pages, then gave it back and moved to the next carriage. After about 15 minutes, the train started up again.

In the dining car, having breakfast, Richard asked the waiter when they would get in to Milan.

"Cinq heures. Peut-etre six."

So, early to mid-afternoon. Again, he sat on in the car after finishing his meal. In the distance, further down the valley, he could see bluish-plains.

Moving across the flatland, the train passed a number of

villages, then stopped briefly at a small town. By now, the open country was diminishing, and there were more roads and houses. Gradually, the houses spread toward the horizon, and, when they reached it, Richard knew the train was now in Milan's suburbs.

Passing into the shadow of Milan station, he looked up to the roof, and it reminded him of those of some of the London terminals, such as Paddington and Victoria: high, a double parabola, meshed with girders. The sounds of engines and voices echoed against it and against the station walls.

He made his way to the platform exit, where he finally surrendered the ticket he had kept in a safe place since leaving London. In a gesture which was over barely before he could think about it, he passed it to the sprucely-uniformed collector who briefly scrutinised it, nodded his head, then looked at the person behind him.

The passenger area was crowded. It had a neon-signed bar and cafe on one side, a couple of bookstalls, a stationer's, and some small shops. The ticket offices were on the opposite side. As he moved his eyes across the wide distance from one side to the other, he reflected that the station was almost as big as Victoria or Paddington, and was the kind of huge steel and concrete structure that had previously been associated in his mind more with industrial Britain than with Italy. But he remembered what he had heard about Milan's being a commercial city, and realised he should not be surprised at such in-ornateness.

At the stationer's, summoning up his small knowledge of Italian, he bought a map of the city.

On the station steps, he looked across a car-filled square to a wide, thin skyscraper with the word 'Fiat' across the top. He could see, through its windows, hundreds of strips of fluorescent lighting. Around the square were other office buildings, and leading off it were multi-laned roads with lots of vehicles travelling fast, toward and away from the city centre, which he discerned as a high, bluish ridge whose vague outline was broken at various points by the roofs of nearer buildings.

Where to go now? He had to find a place to stay for the night. Memories of his arrival in Lisbon returned briefly. He knew that the Italian for 'pensao' was 'pensione', and decided, as in Lisbon, to enlist the services of a taxi driver. He walked down the station steps and across the wide pavement to the roadside, the weight of his luggage putting pressure on the join between his forearm and upper arm. A black car with the sign 'taxi' was turning, with a number of other cars, in his direction. Now almost at the kerb, he raised his arm, in the hope that the driver would see him without having a completely clear view. He was pleased to see the vehicle slow and pull over.

When the driver put his head out of the window, Richard again tried out his Italian by asking him if he knew of a fairly cheap pensione. He was relieved when the man nodded in apparent comprehension.

As they left the main road and moved through side streets, Richard began to see small buildings which were not contemporary in design; they had orange-tile roofs, white plaster walls, balconies and window shutters; they clearly represented an older Milan. He also passed a number of small churches that dated from various periods in the past. He felt more relaxed among these older buildings, even though they sometimes gave way to huge, anonymous housing estates which reminded him of the ones which had been built in London after slum clearance.

The car stopped in a side street. Richard glanced up and saw a sign saying 'Pensione Alberghi'. The driver looked round to him, and pointed to his metre. As Richard paid him, he wondered how much other custom he bought to the pensione.

Richard booked in, and arranged to pay by the night. In his room, he unpacked. After having a meal in the pensione's dining room, he studied the map he had bought, and worked out where he was now in relation to the school. Tomorrow, when he was due to report, he would have to make his way to the Via Monte Napoleone, where the school was located. This name had previously struck him as distinctive; and remembering his school studies in history, he now thought it probably derived from Napoleon's occupation of Milan during his Italian campaign.

Later, he decided to go out to a cafe for a cup of coffee. There was one just along the road. Inside were only a few people. At a table near the door sat a tall, well-built young man, probably in his late twenties or early thirties, wearing a shiny black leather jacket and a metal bracelet on each wrist. Next to him was a girl, heavily made up, in her early or mid-twenties. The neck-line of her dress was low enough for Richard to see the cleft of her breasts. She was leaning toward the man across the table, saying something to him, and he nodded as he sipped his coffee.

Another girl came in, also with heavy make-up, and went across to their table. The man smiled at her approach, and the girl handed him what looked like some folded bank notes, which he quickly put in the inside pocket of his jacket. The girl sat down, and the man gave her a cigarette, lighting it for her. He then said something to the girl who was already seated, and she got up and went out.

Richard's eyes went to the cafe owner, who was sitting behind the counter looking at the table by the door and drawing on a cigarette. Richard felt clear about what was going on at the table, and assumed the young man had an arrangement with the cafe owner. He finished his coffee and walked out into the sharp light of the high-up street lamp, to return to the pensione. What he had just seen was, he realised, part of his introduction to Milan.

CHAPTER TWENTY

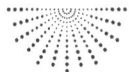

THE NEXT MORNING, RICHARD FOUND HIMSELF IN THE MIDDLE OF THE city's rush hour as he made his way to the school. The long tram he had boarded quickly became crowded, and was soon in a traffic jam on one of the main roads. As it moved slowly along, he saw a number of office buildings which looked as if they dated from the 1920s and 30s, because they were in the same heavily neo-classical style he had noted of a number of buildings in London constructed in the inter-war years.

Checking his map, he saw that Via Monte Napoleone was four turnings on the left from where they were now, and he began edging his way through the line of standing passengers so as to be at the exit door in good time.

Via Monte Napoleone was a fairly narrow street, but had a sophisticated look. It contained a jeweller's, a furrier's, a small art gallery and an expensive confectioner's. There was also a bank and a small hotel. It seemed a contrast to the tawdriness he had seen the night before, but he wondered, in passing, how wide the difference really was. Customers for prostitutes might just as easily be found in this locality as in any other.

About a third of the way along the street, he saw the sign 'The British School' and mounted the steps to the entrance.

Again, brief memories of Lisbon returned to him, and he now noted that the foyer was of similar size to that of the Lisbon school.

In the secretary's office, he was told that the Principal was expecting him and would be arriving shortly. He waited on one of the foyer seats.

After about ten minutes, a tall, fair-haired man about forty, wearing a sports jacket and a very colourful tie, came into the foyer, glanced in Richard's direction, then went into the secretary's office. About half a minute later, he re-appeared, now looking across at Richard with a broad smile. He walked over, hand extended.

"Richard? Richard Lane?" with an American accent.

"Yes," slightly surprised at the accent, but at the same time realising there was no good reason to be.

"So glad you're here. Richard. I'm Andrew Stephens."

As Richard shook his hand, he noticed his eyes, looking down from a height, pass over his hair and forehead.

"Shall we go into my office?"

The seats in the office were plush black leather, and there were expensive-looking draperies over the windows. Richard wondered what Stephen's salary might be, and for a moment thought of Simpson in Lisbon; but he reflected that any comparison had to be in the light of the fact that general living standards were much higher in Italy than in Portugal.

"Please sit down," smiled Stephens, now behind his mahogany desk.

They began discussing teaching arrangements and salary. As they spoke, Richard again noticed Stephens's eyes pass over his hair and forehead, and now over the whole of his face. He found he had no disagreements with what Stephens was saying: the teaching hours were well distributed throughout the week, and the salary appeared to be quite adequate.

"Well, Richard, it looks as if we've got everything sorted out." Then, "By the way, where are you staying at the moment?"

Richard gave him details, explaining that he soon planned to find somewhere permanent.

"So," said Stephens, "you're not fully settled in yet."

Then he opened a small brown box on his desk. "Cigarette?"

"No, thanks. I don't smoke."

Stephens took one for himself and lit it. "Look, if there's any help I can give you – seeing as you're just off the boat, so to speak – I'll be most willing to." He smiled again, now more broadly, and Richard saw a gold filling in one of his side-teeth. "We could meet for a drink one evening, perhaps – to talk about any problems you may have. Better yet, you could come round to my place."

Noting the suddenness of the suggestion, and the bright orange-and-blue of Stephens's tie, Richard replied, "Thanks. I'll let you know."

Stephen's eyes fixed opaquely on his for a moment, the smile contracting a little. "All right," he said less audibly.

Conversation continued for a minute or so. Then Stephens was opening the door for him. Walking across the foyer to the exit, Richard smiled slightly to himself, reflecting on Stephens's invitation.

Because he was due to start teaching the following Monday, he decided to try and find permanent accommodation by the end of the week. He made enquiries at the Pensione; the management didn't know of anywhere, but suggested an information service that was situated near the station. Next morning, he took a tram, and was pleasantly surprised to find that the service's staff spoke English fluently. Two or three addresses were suggested to him; one, he was told, wasn't an apartment but a room in a family house, and therefore going at a very cheap rate. He took the addresses, and decided to try the cheap one first. From his map, he saw that the location was on the outskirts of town, near the San Siro soccer stadium, which he knew was the home of the Milan team. The tram journey covered quite some time. He went through the city centre, and into the older parts of town which he had not seen before, including a number of finely designed piazzas. At one point, he saw in the distance what he took to be the spire of Milan Cathedral. Eventually, the buildings, now mainly houses, became more spread out, and the traffic thinner. The large housing estates, which he had seen previously, re-appeared. He got off the tram a road away from the one he was looking for. When he came to the house number, he double-checked it from the address sheet, then pressed the bell.

The door opened and a plump, shortish, middle-aged woman, wearing a plain pinafore over a short-sleeved frock, was standing looking at him with a slight, inquiring smile. Her height and build immediately reminded him of Pina: this, perhaps, was what Pina would look like in her 40s or 50s.

"Si, signor?" her brown eyes expressing both warmth and curiosity. Bringing his Italian once more into play, he referred to the information service, and explained he had just arrived in Milan. She began nodding before he could finish his slowly-worded sentence, her smile now fuller, and gestured for him to come in.

The room to let was on the first floor, well away from the sound of the woman's family, who occupied the ground floor. He did not know how much family she had, but, on the way up, had heard three different voices – all young adult – coming from the large kitchen at the end of the passageway. She pulled open the window curtains with quick movements of her plump arms, the flesh shaking above the elbows; then she drew down the bedspread on the bed. Richard found it hard to imagine her without a family.

Her smile still full, she moved her arm in a quarter-circle, to emphasise how spacious the room was; then showed him the sink, with hot and cold running water, and the view from the window. Watching her gestures, he noted that her hands were small in proportion to the width of her arms: smaller, in fact, than Pina's. He found himself wanting to stay in sight of her, day by day.

To confirm the figure he had been given by the information service, he asked what the rent was. Her answer chimed with what he had been told, and he said he would take the room.

"Buono," she replied, "buono."

He made arrangements to move in that evening, and she gave him the keys, for when he would be returning.

The transfer was relatively simple, and the cost of the taxi across town was less than he thought it would be.

CHAPTER TWENTY-ONE

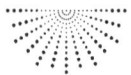

THE FOLLOWING MONDAY, RICHARD HAD THREE CLASSES, OF MIXED ages. The students were animated, but in one class, which was almost entirely female, there was a girl who sat away from the others. She was extremely thin and pale, and also diminutive. Her light brown hair was scant. She rarely spoke, and Richard noticed that, when asked to answer a question, she became slightly tense. He had the impression she did not want to be looked at by the other students. At one stage in the lesson, he asked a question which no one was able to answer, and he turned to the girl. She gave the correct reply. From the other side of the room, a girl with lustrous, elaborately-styled brown hair and full, pink-painted lips, called out, "Ah, one of her boyfriends must be English." Several other girls laughed. The diminutive girl flushed slightly, swallowed, then said "O-ooh," without looking at the others, as if used to such comments, and lowered her eyes to her notebook. Richard continued the lesson; whenever the girl with pink-painted lips spoke, he listened without expression.

During the course of the day, he passed Stephens twice in the foyer, at a distance, and the latter smiled briefly before moving on. Richard nodded in reply, feeling that Stephens would not again ask him to meet for a drink.

In the evening, returning to his lodgings on the tram, he thought about the isolated girl in the class. There was, he realised, a very real possibility that she would never have a boyfriend. Once again, general thoughts about sexual loneliness went through his mind.

At his lodgings, his landlady smiled her full smile from the kitchen, a tea-towel hanging over her forearm. He returned the smile, picturing her spending almost all of the day in the house, cooking, cleaning, and doing other chores for her family. Then, once more, he thought about the girl in the class.

After going out for a meal at a local trattoria, he wrote to his mother and Paul, giving them his address. As he sealed the envelopes, his mind returned to Pina. Gazing down at the circle of light the lamp made on the surface of his table, he again felt he was right in the decision he had taken, despite the immediate emotional consequences that decision would have for her.

The teaching continued, without any major problems. In addition to working at the school, he got an extra class in business and commercial English at a large factory on the outskirts of the city. The days were falling into a regular pattern, and he liked the variety of travelling by tram to school and by metro to the factory.

But the sense of security that came with establishing a regular work routine was partly undermined by the absence of sexual satisfaction. Frustration was his familiar travelling companion, he wryly reflected. He resumed masturbating; images of Audrey and Jill returned to him, as if irresistibly, as his breathing quickened in the dark.

One morning, in the school staffroom, he was sitting alone, making notes in preparation for a class, when a young woman came in whom he had not seen before. Her brown hair was done in a bun, and she had slightly aquiline features, with a rather long nose. Her skin was reddish, with a few spots. Her pale-blue eyes were small but bright and perceptive-looking. He was not physically attracted to her but liked the way she smiled to him as she sat down at the other end of the room. He returned the smile, wanting to get into conversation with her. He did not know her nationality, but had a sense that she was English.

She had opened a book, and now she looked up, seeing his gaze before he could avert it. Again she smiled.

"Good book?" he ventured in English.

"Yes, it is. A history of the Risorgimento."

So, she was English. Her accent was actually north-of-England. He immediately recalled from the history he had done at school that the Risorgimento was the intellectual and radical movement which emerged in Italy in the early to mid-nineteenth century, and which challenged the political *status quo*.

"Do you," he asked, "have a special interest in history?"

"Well, Italian history. I thought that, since I am living here, I should learn more about the country's background and culture."

"I should too." Then, "Sometimes, English teachers think that all they have to do is go to another country and bestow the privilege of learning English on the natives. They're the ones who aren't interested in the country itself – at least not in its history."

"Yes, that's certainly true of some. Have you taught abroad before?"

"In Portugal. Lisbon. I was there for a year. Learnt quite a lot about the country's political situation." Then, "And you?"

"This is my first time abroad."

"You're from the north of England, aren't you?"

"Ah, you could tell by my accent. Yes, from Sheffield."

"I'm a Londoner. My name's Richard."

"Margaret."

"How long have you been in Milan?"

"This is my second year." Again, she smiled, but now only slightly, and her eyes momentarily lowered to the book cover.

When she raised them, she asked, "Are you here by yourself?"

"Yes."

"So am I."

He broke the silence which followed with, "How long do you plan to stay?"

"I'm not sure. Probably to the end of the year." Then, "Actually, my first year was quite difficult. I didn't get the number of classes I'd been promised, and my salary was reduced. I was living just on a plate of spaghetti or pasta each day or every other day. Prices are high here."

"What about accommodation?"

"That I could barely afford. I was staying in a pensione at first; then I moved to a very small flat."

"And how are things now?"

"Oh, I have enough classes. Things are okay, financially."

"But you still think you'll go home at the end of the year?"

She nodded. "Perhaps Milan wasn't quite the best choice as a place to teach in Italy. It's a big city where everyone's in a hurry-- rather like Sheffield, or maybe London."

"Certainly like London."

"And so a bit difficult for people who are…" trailing off.

"Who are what?"

Her face had flushed a little. "Oh, I shouldn't have said it really."

"No, go on."

"Well, a bit shy."

"Yes, that's right," he said after a moment. "The big city is harder if you're not extraverted."

She asked, "Do you have that problem too?"

"To some extent," but now thinking mainly of Paul.

"Yes, I suppose a lot of people do. It's basically a difference of degree,"

Still thinking mainly of Paul, he asked, "Why did you decide to come abroad?"

"Oh, restlessness. Seeking something new."

He decided to ask, "Didn't you think your shyness would bring difficulties?"

"Yes, but I was willing to take the chance, to see how things turned out."

"What," he went on, "do you think you'll do when you return to England?"

"I'm not sure. Perhaps do some further study. But I don't know."

Just then, another female member of staff came into the room. Margaret looked up at her, smiled briefly, then glanced at her wristwatch. She said to Richard, "Actually, I have to be going. I've got a class."

He nodded. He didn't know exactly what to say; he was interested in seeing her again but, because he was not attracted to her, did not want to ask her out.

As she picked up her things, she smilingly glanced at him. He wondered if she was attracted to him; if she was, this would be an additional reason for not asking her out. Still he did not know what to say, and smiled back perfunctorily. Then he managed: "So, be seeing you."

"Yes," now smiling in a slightly strained way. She left the room.

CHAPTER TWENTY-TWO

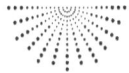

WITH HER BROAD SMILE, THE LANDLADY HANDED HIM TWO LETTERS. Immediately, he recognised the handwriting: his mother's and Paul's. Opening his mother's letter first, he read how glad she was that he was settled into his new job. Was he eating well? Was the place he was staying in warm at night? He smiled at the familiar enquiries. He quickly wrote a letter to reassure her on both these points, and gave her some of his impressions of Milan.

Paul had found a job with a charity organisation giving counselling help to people with drink and drugs problems. He didn't, he explained, actually give advice, because that required special training, but was involved in processing information and compiling case files on people who sought help. He had two assistants working under him, and made decisions on what final shape the case file would take before it went to the counsellor for use in working with the client. He enjoyed the job, he said, because it exercised his capacity for mentally organising and summarising facts and figures, an ability which had been activated in a different way by his accountancy work. He also enjoyed the work because it gave him insight into other people's problems. He now saw that a number of the fears and anxieties he had experienced in the past were not unique to him, and it was a big relief to realise this.

He added that Freda was still very supportive, and that she had, in fact, been more so to him than he to her; but he would now try to even the scales. He then said he had asked her to marry him, and that she had consented.

Richard wrote back to Paul, congratulating him on Freda's consent, and on his new job. While noting Paul's point about discovering he had not been alone in experiencing certain kinds of apprehensiveness, he decided not to make any comment on it; Paul was clear about it, so nothing more needed to be said.

The weeks passed, and Richard did not see Margaret again in the staffroom. In fact, he rarely saw one teacher more than twice, and realised that the staff set-up here was far more impersonal than in Lisbon; so much so, that he even regretted the absence of jarring incidents, such as the one with Jennie. The lack of personal contact seemed to him a pity, since there was quite a variety of staff – Americans, English, French and German; but most people came in just to give their lessons, then disappeared into the vastness of the city.

He started walking round the city at weekends, letting his curiosity take him from street to street. He noted more of the inter-war architecture he had seen on first arriving: banks, insurance offices, commercial houses. As he walked, faces passed either side of him, singly or in clusters. He noted many instances of virtual expressionlessness; also, similarities in the angles in which eyes were directed at the space ahead. He started to feel what he had previously experienced in London and Lisbon; a sense of mass-averageness, of something pervasively middling. He sat in cafes and trattoria, and the impression was reinforced.

He then began to think about his activity as a language teacher, and how intellectually limited it was. True, it provided opportunities for working abroad, but he now realised he could not continue with it indefinitely.

What, then, about other activities? There was the writing project he had discussed with Ray: the search for the essence of the physical world, a search that could not be aided by religious belief. As he once again pondered the complexities of the task, he experienced a slight contraction in his stomach: this was something he just had to attempt--to fill an emptiness that must be ended; yet he did not know if he would succeed.

Such uncertainty and suspense must, he realised, be common to many people like himself who had decided to try and build up a general picture of things from scratch, without the help of any articles of faith. Again, his mind turned to the most thoughtful people of the generation preceding his – those born in the 1920s – and he tried to imagine their feelings in a cultural situation similar to his own; likewise, the feelings of the most thoughtful people of the generation before that.

If he was going to make a start, he would have to do more reading in science and philosophy, but that would not be easy in Milan, since there was little access to English language books. He must wait, then, till he returned to England.

One Sunday, he visited Milan Cathedral, and was immediately struck by the rich intricacy of its Gothic architecture: with its greyish-blue main spire, and, behind it, the miniature spires, turrets and gargoyles ranged along the Cathedral's roof. In front of the building was a huge piazza, skirted by cafes and shops. There were lots of pigeons, and he was reminded of Trafalgar Square in London. As his eye scanned the spire, and the detailed stone carvings around the high door which led into the building, his admiration awoke the memory of the church near his home in London: the church which had held his interest at a time when he had felt estranged from most of the locality. He recalled that it had interested him because, even though he had rejected religion, it seemed part of the answer to his question about the fundamental nature of things. Now, he felt the Cathedral was also part of the answer. But how exactly, he was not clear. Why were churches relevant to a non-religious enquiry?

An answer glimmered: because the outstanding artistic quality of at least some churches, like that of great paintings, poems, novels and symphonies, was a product of human capacity—the capacity, at any rate, of a few. So, the high spire, no matter how far it reached into the air, brought the mind back to the people who made it, to their powers. And what was the source of these powers? This was one of the basic questions which now had to be answered.

The thought recurred that great works of art were the achievement of a minority. He remembered his conversation with Ray about most people's lack of radical originality and creativity, and therefore their lack of desire to try out something on their own.

Then his mind went to his landlady – the 'signora', as he now called her. Here was someone who had followed a normal course of life: raising children, tending constantly to their needs, keeping house for them. He recalled a recent occasion when he had seen her coming back from shopping, flanked by her two teenage sons, each carrying a heavy bag while she carried a lighter one. Her fatness had meant that she'd had to take slow steps, steps made even slower by the raised-heel shoes that she wore instead of her usual slippers. Yet, despite a certain awkwardness in walking, her face beamed with satisfaction at having her two sons beside her. She had sought no sources of fulfilment beyond the normal biological roles of wife and mother, and was evidently completely happy in that choice. The uncomplicated pleasure she derived from it gave her a very prepossessing quality, and this fact reminded Richard that to be likeable you did not have to be unusual or original—a pioneer in the arts or sciences, or anything like that.

Yet this kind of prepossessing quality could, he felt, be of only limited interest. It was, in a way, like Harry's attractive easy-going'ness: engaging up to a point, but, after that, not a subject for a searching mind to focus on. Such a mind had to centre on uncommon areas of experience, areas hard to penetrate, and ones which the signora would in fact not comprehend. Her mental world lay only on their margins.

CHAPTER TWENTY-THREE

HE REVISITED THE CATHEDRAL, AND GOT TO KNOW IT WELL, BOTH ITS exterior and interior. He went to other historical sites in the city, and also became familiar with an area near the cathedral which contained a number or small art galleries. But eventually, he wanted to see the areas outside the city. He knew that Lake Como and other lakes were situated fairly near, and one Saturday took a trip to Como.

It was an attractive resort, he felt, with lots of villas along the lakeside and a profusion of yachts on the water. But the surrounding area was simply hilly – with no mountains. He had been told that mountains, the beginnings of the Italian Alps, lay further north. On a subsequent visit, he set off by bus as soon as he got to Como, heading for the next lake along: Maggiore. Well before arriving, he could see in the distance the indigo of mountains, their peaks white. His breathing quickened slightly: he was reminded of his train journey through the French Alps into Italy.

The town of Maggiore was smaller than Como, less geared to tourism, and had a basic quietness that Como lacked. Also, there were fewer vessels on the lake, and he could trace the ways the breeze scored its surface over wide areas. Looking across the water to the mountains, he reflected that, beyond the peaks, lay three countries: France, Germany and Switzerland. The air was so clear that nothing in the outline of the mountains was obscured.

He started to feel – for the first time, he realised –that he was fully situated in Europe. He had not had this feeling in Portugal, perhaps because of its extraordinarily bad social conditions and its position on the western edge of the Continent. Now, he experienced the emotion as a sense of being more than just British, and recalled the interest that had been awakened in him by French and German writers. He thought of other national literatures and cultures that waited to be explored: in addition to the French and German, there were the Italian, Spanish, Russian, and others. With his eyes still fixed on the mountains, he had a longing to be enriched by the best these cultures could offer, and in this way to be fully European: fully so, he now comprehended, by sifting for a kind of cultural gold, a kind of thing in which the majority of people displayed no extensive interest.

As he walked along the lake's edge, he thought of Margaret, and her attempt to get to know about Italian history and culture. He wondered if she felt the same way he did about Europe, and briefly considered that, unless he saw her again, he would never know.

He realised there would not be time that day both to explore Maggiore and go up in to the mountains; and decided that, to do the latter, he would immediately get a bus from Maggiore on his next visit.

As the mountains beyond Maggiore got nearer, Richard could distinguish small chalets on the lower slopes, and tree copses. The bus engine made slight heaving sounds as it tackled the steepening gradient of the road. At the top of the slope, another lake came into view, much smaller than Maggiore, and with only a few buildings at its edge.

When the bus descended to the lake and stopped, he bought a bottle of beer and a sandwich at the only cafe. He then started on foot up the nearest mountain road.

Occasionally, a car passed him, but otherwise the only sounds were those of the wind being sieved by the leaves of the trees which lined the road, and the whistling of birds. The further up he went, the hotter the sun seemed to be. He began to sweat slightly.

He looked down at the blue-grey lake, and could now see its total shape: like a comma, magnified and viewed sideways. Up ahead, above the tree-line, was a snow peak, less pointed at its apex than it had seemed from further down, and not quite as high on the horizon as he had earlier expected. No sound came from it, and nothing but snow could be seen on it. Gazing at its size and singleness, as the sweat cooled on his forehead, he was curiously calm and restful, feeling he was acquiring something of its steadfastness. The words, 'Lone as a peak in Darien' passed through his mind, and he remembered that this was a phrase from Milton. The long vowel sounds, he mused, helped to convey the appropriate image of majestic isolation.

Isolation. Did this word apply to him too? If so, was he seeking steadfastness to fortify him in his solitude? To both questions, the answer was 'Yes'. He was indeed alone, as much as Margaret appeared to be; and he wanted to maintain poise while bearing the weight of aloneness – he did not want to stagger under that weight, either in public or in private.

Just at that moment, he heard a car approaching and looked away from the road so that his facial expression would not be seen. Then, as the car passed, he realised – with a slight smile at his over-carefulness – that the driver would probably not have bothered to look at him even if his face had been visible. He continued up the road, deciding to get some way higher and then rest.

He reached a point where he had an even clearer view of the lake than before. The comma was slightly smaller, though still at the same angle, and now completely blue, reflecting the sky totally.

From it, his eyes turned back to the mountain. Beneath the snow-covered part, the rock was bright brown flecked with mauve as the sun's rays beat down on it. He looked into the mile or so between the silent bareness of the rock's surface and his body.

His mind returned to his writing project; perhaps, he speculated, because the thoughts of isolation had led to those of isolated activity. He reminded himself that he would have to wait till he got back to England before he could start work, and that it was questionable whether he would actually succeed in the task. The latter was a question as open as the space that lay before him.

He heard another car pass behind him, and then its sound fade. Not feeling hungry or thirsty, he decided to watch the slow descent of the sun till it met the mountain at the point which he roughly calculated to be about two thirds up its left slope. He sat down on a small rock by the roadside.

As the sun lowered in imperceptible movements, the flecks of mauve on the rock-mass increased. Gradually, the burning circle neared the slope. When it touched, the light dimmed slightly. He knew that, when it eventually disappeared behind the mountain, it would be gone from sight much earlier than on a flat horizon, and that by late afternoon he would still be seeing the bright light it shed without seeing it. The thought reminded him of his isolation: it gave the idea of his being cut off from something vital and radiant.

But, as the sun became a semi-circle, he recalled his previous ideas about being fully European. These were supportive. They accentuated the fact that, although shadows were being cast across him, he was on a height. From a position of discrimination, he would explore the best that Europe had to offer.

CHAPTER TWENTY-FOUR

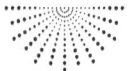

ON HIS WEEKEND WALKS THROUGH THE CITY, HE DISCOVERED A number of churches, built in a variety of styles. These included a large, Romanesque one in auburn brick, with parts of its outer wall frayed and broken. Whereas several of the other churches seemed no more than three hundred or so years old at most, this one was clearly pre-mediaeval. Thinking about this enlarged time-perspective, he realised he had not yet seen any Roman ruins. This surprised him, because he knew from his rather scant knowledge of Italian history that Milan had briefly been the capital city of the Western Empire. He recalled that it had also been of considerable importance in mediaeval times, as well as in later periods such as that of the Napoleonic wars.

Also, he remembered reading that it was near Milan that the dictator Mussolini had been found by the Italian Resistance, trying to escape to Switzerland. He had been shot, and his body displayed in the city centre for all to see.

He paused at the thought of the Resistance. The 'Partigiani', as they were known, had clearly been prominent in Milan, and he wondered what kind of people they were. Many must still be alive – though, it seemed, now socially obscure, like several members of other Resistance movements throughout Europe. He recalled what he had heard about Sartre in France, and wondered who among the Partigiani had distinguished themselves for courage and dedication. The achievements of the European Resistance were, he felt, part of the best that Europe had to offer.

Sitting at a pavement table of a crowded café, he could hear from the cafe's inner area the sound of a pop-song being played on a jukebox. A youthful male voice was struggling through a succession of melodramatic extremes of emotion. He found himself briefly reflecting on the whole pop music industry, as he had encountered it in his school and university years; and he considered the frequently crude way it sought to arouse feeling in its listeners. Across the sound of the pop-song were the voices of people talking, laughing. A young woman holding a cigarette threw her head back and giggled at something her male companion had said. A waiter picked up and pocketed a tip left on a dish at an empty table.

Richard suddenly had a sense of things facile and trivial—things far removed from the searing experiences of the Resistance, many of whose members must have burned through to the deepest self-knowledge by their acts of commitment, choice and decision-making. Their experiences lay only about a quarter of a century back, yet how many people now thought of them?

He recollected previous thoughts he had had about World War II, especially one he had confided to Ray about never having known the intense sense of togetherness which war must have engendered, at least in some. And he remembered Ray's words about those born in the immediate post-war period having arrived too late for that experience.

However, his thoughts then drifted to his own experience, at school and university, and he recalled something else he had thought about the war: that, overall, it must have been a mixed experience, with varying degrees of communication between individuals. Probably, then, the intense sense of togetherness had been far from total; the individual had felt closer to some of his or her contemporaries than to others, and extremely close to just a few. Still, the experience of very deep attachment, though rare, was invaluable; and the general war situation must have increased the opportunities for it.

The large envelope had his mother's handwriting on it. He had been expecting a reply from her, but was curious about the size of the envelope. When he opened it, he saw, with her letter, another envelope with the large-sized handwriting which he immediately recognised as Pina's. He swallowed. Pina had, then, written him a second letter even though he had not answered her first one.

With slow finger movements, he opened Pina's envelope. She was asking him to write and "'tell me something'". He knew this meant she wanted him to confide in her. She added that she was carrying on from day to day in the usual way, "talking to the people," continuing with her job and her English studies. As he read, he received the impression there was still no other man in her life. Also, he recalled the slight lump on her second finger, one similar to his own, that had resulted from the continual pressure of holding a pen against that particular point.

He felt an impulse to reverse his decision not to write, since her need for him was still evident. But then he re-traced the logic behind that decision, and, hard though it was, he re-affirmed it. If he was to do what was best for her-- open her life to somebody else -- then her letter must go unanswered.

He then read his mother's letter, again smiling at the simplicity of her statements, and folded the paper in half. That evening, he wrote a reply.

CHAPTER TWENTY-FIVE

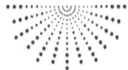

OVER THE NEXT COUPLE OF WEEKS, RICHARD NOTICED A TALLISH, shapely girl spending short periods in the staffroom. He took particular note of her because she was one of the new teachers he saw more than once. He perceived that, when she came in, she had only a little facial make-up; then she would go into the ladies' room and re-appear with face fully made up – not excessively, in his opinion, but sufficiently to highlight her well-formed nose, full lips and high forehead.

He thought her figure had an athletic beauty: small but well-proportioned breasts, slim waist, full hips and legs like those of a slender gymnast or dancer. He knew she was English because he had heard her speak briefly to other members of staff. She smiled readily as she spoke, giving the impression of having a lot of self-confidence. Attracted to her, he began thinking of asking her out.

Physically, she reminded him of Susan at university. He imagined that Harry would have had no trouble attracting her, had he seen and wanted her. This thought had a discouraging effect because he knew that, in matters of this kind, he was no match for Harry, and could not approach the task of making a date with anything like the confidence, regularly reinforced by experience, which Harry could muster. Another discouraging consideration was that perhaps she already had a boyfriend, maybe several.

One afternoon, he entered the staffroom and saw her sitting alone, reading a book, her legs crossed. His stomach tightened: here was his chance, but he had never spoken to her previously, and before anything else he would have to think of a way of starting a conversation. She looked up at him for a moment, then down at her book. Not knowing what image she had of him in her mind, he went over to a chair in the corner of the room and got out some lesson preparation.

A few minutes passed. He looked up. Her head was still down. He decided to ask, in a contrived casual tone, "Are you teaching later today?"

She raised her eyes, and smiled readily, broadly. "Yes, in an hour." As she spoke, she turned a lock of hair behind her ear with her index finger.

Feeling a little encouraged, he continued, "Which level do you teach at?"

"Oh, Intermediate."

His eyes involuntarily went to her legs; but he checked himself and turned them back to hers. There, he thought he saw a hint of an expression of satisfaction.

"And your level?" she asked, still with the smile.

"Intermediate and Advanced."

"'Advanced' sounds very sophisticated."

"It isn't really."

Her eyes remaining on his, she lifted one leg off the other and straightened it, turning her foot slightly. Richard was now sure she could see his attraction to her. He ventured, "I finish teaching at 7.30 tonight. How about you?"

"At eight."

Her eyes now definitely showed satisfaction. He decided to continue: "Would you like to meet for a drink after you finish?"

She suddenly shook her head. "Not possible. It's one of my Masaratis tonight."

He noted the way she put it, and wondered how many boyfriends she had who owned sports cars. Smiling thinly, he inquired, "Does he have this year's model?"

"You bet."

"And which are the other cars in your life?"

She grinned, apparently genuinely amused. "Oh, Ferraris. Porsches."

"What hope, then, for a pedestrian?"

Still she grinned, but said nothing. The realisation came to him that she had just wanted to hear him ask for a date, and that he had become a source of amusement to her. He stood up.

"Well, I have to be off."

"Have fun."

Instead of a verbal reply, he nodded.

Outside the school building, he felt irritated at having left himself exposed. Memories of similar experiences at university came back to him, and with them the feeling that by now he should have been able to foresee possible humiliation and therefore avoid it. He went to a nearby cafe and drank a cup of strong coffee. As his irritation faded, he found himself thinking of Margaret, and how much she contrasted with this other girl – who, it seemed, had never borne the weight of isolation.

Later, after he'd finished teaching, he waited in a shop alcove down the street from the school entrance. At two minutes past eight, a long, low-slung sports car pulled up. A tall, young man with black curly hair spryly got out and went into the school. About five minutes later, he re-appeared, and Richard was not surprised to see who was with him. The girl laughed and threw her head back as the man opened the car door for her. Richard watched the vehicle move down the street and turn the corner.

CHAPTER TWENTY-SIX

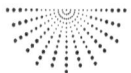

DURING HIS WEEKEND WALKS, HE RETURNED TO THE SIDE STREETS NEAR the Cathedral which contained a range of small art galleries. There were also a number of cafes frequented by local artists, and he spent time in them, drinking coffee and watching the men of various ages––many of the younger ones with beards––who came in carrying sketches and sometimes finished canvases. They would show their work to each other and discuss it. The cafe also hosted a number of prostitutes, again of varying ages; a number of times, they talked with, then left with, the artists. Richard reflected that this was apparently the closest Milan –– emphatically a business city––got to having a Bohemian quarter. Also, he wondered how many of the artists possessed distinctive talent and would make an enduring mark: the kind of mark which the Cathedral, just two streets away, constituted. Again, his thoughts returned to the general theme of human capacities and powers.

As winter set in, snow fell, not as heavily as in England, but still quite plentiful. He got used to seeing white pavements each morning. He had to wear his topcoat because temperatures dropped almost as low as in England. He recalled that, in Portugal, winter had not reminded him of the home country because it had been characterised by rain; umbrellas, not topcoats, had been the requirement there.

He received further letters from his mother and Paul, each with its idiosyncratic qualities, to which he would attune himself when replying. Paul, talking about his job, said the work was continually opening his eyes to things poignant and worth knowing. He then said that Freda and he had decided to marry in the Spring.

Richard penned replies, again congratulating Paul. Later, in bed, he developed an erection and masturbated, thinking of the girl at the school.

Winter gradually turned to Spring, and the weather became as warm as the average English summer. He thought about Paul's approaching wedding, and about what he himself would do when the academic year ended in June. He would not sign another contract with the school and continue for a further session, since he had definitely reached the limits of the intellectual satisfaction to be derived from the kind of teaching he was doing. While determined to start on his writing project as soon as possible, he knew he must get a job of some kind, having no other source of income.

On the appropriate date, Richard sent Paul and Freda a wedding card. Paul promptly replied by letter, thanking him and saying the wedding had gone well. He and Freda were now renting a flat in Ilford.

With the arrival of summer, the weather grew even hotter. His teaching was coming to a successful conclusion. Also, he had saved enough money to take a holiday before returning to England. He would, he decided, go to Rome.

As he shook hands with Stephens at the end of his last day of teaching, he noted the latter's forced smile: the skin was crinkled at the corners of his mouth and his eyes had an opaquely genial expression as they looked down at him.

Walking across the foyer to the exit, he briefly felt regret that he had not seen Margaret again.

That night, he wrote again to his mother and Paul, explaining that he would soon be leaving Milan and that they should not send any more letters to the Milan address.

CHAPTER TWENTY-SEVEN

THE SIGNORA'S SMILE WAS BROAD AND FULL, HER HEAD SLIGHTLY inclined, as he stood in the passageway with his two suitcases. Wearing her customary apron, she held out her small hand and he shook it. When he told her he was going to Rome, she enthused that she had once been there, just after the war. As he crossed the courtyard in the early morning light, she waved, the flesh on her upper arm shaking.

Moving once again under the massive roof girders of the railway station, he perspired as his eyes searched the indicator board for the departure time of the Rome train. He then made his way to the platform, found the train half full, and got into one of the middle carriages.

As the train passed through the city's suburbs, he saw the floodlight towers of the San Siro soccer stadium, and smiled slightly with the recollection that he had never got round to watching the Milan team play. He remembered that in Portugal he had not watched the Lisbon team either.

The train entered open country, and he noted that the land was flatter than to the north of Milan: wide, level fields and, frequently, cypress trees. As the morning progressed the heat increased, and, with the consent of the other passengers, he pulled the carriage window down full.

Across the afternoon, the train stopped at a number of small towns, and on three occasions Richard bought cold drinks from vendors on the platforms. With the approach of evening, the air became cooler. As night fell, there was a build-up of suburbs; he knew they were coming into Rome.

Clusters of lights showed through the window; but, because of the darkness, it was difficult to judge distances. When the train pulled into the station, Richard immediately noted that it was smaller than Milan's. He yawned, feeling heat-fatigue after his long journey; he did not want to go out into the city now, but find a place to stay. He saw that the station waiting-room was large, and decided he would spend the night there. After having some coffee and pastrami rolls at a snack-stand, he found a place in the corner of the waiting room, and wedged his cases in the space underneath his seat and against the wall. This way, they would be protected by his legs in their sitting position.

He hoped he would stay awake through the night, but found himself dozing intermittently. By dawn, he was fully awake and was pleased to find that he felt fairly fresh. The station toilets were almost empty and he used one of the basins to wash and shave.

He again bought coffee at the snack-stand. By now, the sun was up, and the bars of light which spanned the station walls were bright. He walked out into the sunlight and moved his eyes slowly from left to right and back again. In the distance, against a pale blue sky, was an elevated horizon: one of the seven hills on which he knew Rome was built. The buildings were generally much older than those in Milan: a profusion of orange-tiled roofs and white walls filling the hillside, interspersed with greenery, especially cypress trees. Immediately ahead of him was a main road, wide and very modern, with tall, futuristic-looking street-lamps, but this foreground did not detract from the background: his predominant impression was of the past, as he reflected that some of the Roman-style houses might actually date from Roman times, and that the style had probably been followed continuously since that period.

He recalled enough about Rome from his History lessons at school to know there was a great deal to see: the Coliseum, St Peter's, the palace of King Victor Emmanuel, and many other things. This was one of the oldest cities in the world —'the Eternal City', as he had seen it described: older than London, Paris, Berlin or Moscow.

But before he could do any sight-seeing, he must find a place to stay. He returned to the station and inquired if there was a local tourist information centre. The answer was 'Yes', and he was given directions. He took a tram. At the centre, he was provided with details about a number of inexpensive pensioni. One in particular was recommended to him; it was in a nearby square. Deciding to try it, he took the address, along with a general map of Rome that was offered to him, and made his way there.

The square was away from the main streets, and was quiet. He spotted in one corner, the ruins of a building which appeared to be Roman: a column of Corinthian design; part of a wall; and, on the ground, pieces of a wall-frieze which had collapsed. The stone was a pale yellow but had once, he imagined, been white. The humorous thought struck him that the ruins had been specially placed there, for picturesque effect; but then it occurred to him that, if they were in a quiet area like this, the city must be filled with them.

He looked round at the rest of the square, and saw small houses which appeared to date mostly from the 18th and 19th centuries. These, he then saw, included the Pensione.

Having checked in and unpacked his luggage, he had some breakfast in the Pensione dining room, and then consulted his map to find the quickest way to the Coliseum.

On the tram, he noticed more parts of old buildings on street corners and intersections.

∼

The huge, multi-tiered curve stood in the distance, on the far side of a busy road that encircled it. Richard quickly found that crossing the road was no easy matter. There were no zebra crossings or lights, and the cars were fast. He had to run part of the way to keep a safe distance from some of the vehicles. Eventually, safe on the pavement, he wiped the perspiration from his forehead and looked up. The grey wall of the Coliseum rose high above him, punctuated with arched apertures. Beyond this wall, he knew, untold numbers had met their deaths in front of callous crowds: gladiators, early Christians and others. But other activities had taken place here too: sports events, chariot races – things one could have a positive response to.

Inside the walls, Richard was surprised to find only a few visitors, but then remembered that it was still quite early in the morning, Around him were ranged the levels of stone seating, frayed and in some places crumbled; now empty, but once packed with roaring spectators. He looked across to the flat, sand-surfaced area, also empty, and realised he couldn't begin to imagine how much agony had been experienced there, by stricken gladiators and people mauled by lions and other wild animals. How much blood had soaked without trace into this ground?

He contrasted the spectacles of cruelty with the sports events, and then thought about other positive aspects of Roman culture: the legal system, the achievements in civil engineering, the complexities of the Latin language, the great poets and historians. It was, like most social phenomena, a mixed picture, about which single judgements could not be made. Certainly the picture contained some of the best things Europe had to offer, as well as, undeniably, some of the worst.

He saw, at one side of the arena area, a small café built into the main wall. He couldn't help feeling a sense of irony: three or four people were sipping coffee only a few yards from where thousands had writhed in dying gasps. The thought gave him a sense of the cruel arbitrariness of circumstances: throughout history, countless numbers of innocent people had found themselves in hellish situations from which there was no escape – and that, he realised, was still the case in some parts of the world today. For a moment, he thought about the Portuguese slums and prisons.

More visitors were now appearing, and the voice-level was rising. Richard found it less easy to focus his thoughts.

Outside the Coliseum, he managed to re-cross the road safely. He took another tram, to the Palace of Victor Emmanuel II. Situated on a high point of the city, the white marble edifice commanded a view of three of Rome's hills, and his first visual impression of the city was now amplified: there was much more orange and white, and much more dark green.

The palace itself struck him as artificial. It seemed a late 19th century attempt to present a new version of the classical architectural style, and the result, in his view, was something characterless.

Disappointed, though pleased with the background view, he decided to go and have something to eat. Over a rather heavy pasta lunch in a small trattoria, he made up his mind to leave his visit to the Vatican till the following day, so that he could give himself maximum time for it.

CHAPTER TWENTY-EIGHT

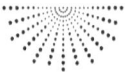

THE SUN SHONE BRIGHTLY ON THE DARK BLUE STONE OF ST PETER'S Square. Richard's eyes moved round the perimeter of the Square and the tall columns which flanked it. Ahead was the dome of St Peter's—immediately reminding him of St Paul's in London; he noted the similarity in general architectural style between the two buildings, while realising that St Peter's was bigger. He also saw that its dome was green, whereas St Paul's was blue-grey. The Cathedral and the Square had, he knew, been designed by Michelangelo.

Going through the Cathedral's massive doors, he passed from sunlight into half-shadow, and his gaze immediately settled on a central column of polished wood, thick as an oak tree, with a spiral design that rose as high into the shadow of the dome as his eyes could trace. At ground level, spread across the huge floor area, were robed statues, tombs, small monuments and, in cavities in the walls, lines of busts. The figures, Richard concluded, would be of leading people in Christian history, principally the history of Catholicism. Unable to recognise any of them, he became acutely aware of his ignorance in this field.

From the far side of the floor, he heard the faint sound of chanting; as he moved across, his eyes distinguished a line of seated priests in brown garments singing from hymn books. Beyond them was a long altar glistening with the flickers of well over a hundred candles. While struck by the lighting effects produced by the candles, Richard noticed, at one end of the line of singers, a priest picking his nose. He smiled at this tiny pocket of triviality amid grandeur.

"Capella Sistina?" echoed a young priest, in response to Richard's question, and pointed toward the end of the Square. Walking toward the Sistine Chapel, Richard reminded himself that this too had been designed by Michelangelo. He also knew that the town of Florence was almost filled with the artist's works, including the statue of David.

As he entered the Chapel, a tourist party was being led in by a guide speaking German. Richard took an information pamphlet from a shelf inside the door and followed the party into a space the size of a large hall, filled with pale light coming through heavily latticed windows. His ear caught the strong guttural sounds of the guide's voice; and, when the guide emphatically pointed upwards, he looked up too.

Above him was a mass of colour and human figures. His eyes tried to take everything in at once, but this was impossible. Also, he began to feel the pressure from craning his neck. He looked down at his pamphlet, which was printed in four languages, and read in the English part that the ceiling painting was Michelangelo's depiction of the major events in the Bible. Again he craned his neck, focussing on the central part of the ceiling. He was struck by the unfailingly precise draughtsmanship of the figures and wondered how the artist had achieved this, painting above his own head. Once more, he looked at the pamphlet, which told him that Michelangelo had worked lying on his back, on wooden boards supported by scaffolding. 'On his back', thought Richard to himself. So his arm was working vertically, with the blood-flow tending downward. He bent his head, eyes dilated. Then, with a succession of head-raises, his eyes eventually covered every main detail of the Biblical panorama.

The guided party were now standing by one of the walls; again, the guide's gutturals reached Richard's ear. He walked over and directed his gaze to what the party were looking at: a wall-high depiction of naked bodies locked in a downward cascade. Again, Richard found the draughtsmanship superb. He read from his pamphlet that this was Michelangelo's 'Last Judgement'; he studied each tortured figure, wondering what kinds of predicaments the artist had had in mind as he had composed. Self-destroying criminality, unassuageable guilt, irreversible error?

As he thought about the artist's mastery in painting, architecture and sculpture, he felt no surprise that the question now recurred to him about the source of such capacity.

The following morning, he posted an air-mail letter to his mother, telling her he would be home in four days. Then he spent the day just walking around the city's side streets, avoiding the main roads. In many places, there were reminders of the past: a column, a piece of wall, or some other remnant-- classical, Romanesque, mediaeval, baroque, and later styles. Frequently, in piazzas, he came across small, ornate fountains that seemed to date from the 17th or 18th centuries; many were working, their small jets ending in a tiny dance of water as droplets emerging from the top of the jet continuously replaced others falling downward.

It was clear that the architecture reflected much of European history, the range of styles serving as an index to its political, religious and cultural changes. Was there another continent, he wondered, with so rich a history? Or, at any rate, another area as relatively small with so varied a past? If one counted ancient Greece, whose architectural influence was evident all around, then that history went back a good three thousand years; and how much had happened in that period in this corner of the globe! Even in just a few countries in this corner – Greece, Italy, France, Germany and Britain – how much had transpired! An image came to him of a profusion of precious stones, catching the light in numberless different ways.

Though, he then reflected, historic feats had been the work of minorities in the European populations, those minorities, added together across three millennia, amounted to a very large number of people: a number displaying tremendous creative energy and power of mind. Again, he bent his head, in contemplation of this power.

Fastening his suitcases, he considered that, if he'd had more money, he would have stayed in Rome longer, and maybe visited Florence.

He took a taxi to the station. On arrival, he found that his train was a little late. He had a cup of coffee at the snack-stand he had used when he first came. The train pulled in; he went to his seat.

'So, back, finally, to London,' he thought, as his carriage jolted into movement.

CHAPTER TWENTY-NINE

The sky was sunny as the train sped past lush green fields toward London. Once more, he was coming home after a period of working abroad, but now he could not envisage another such period, at least not as a teacher of English as a Foreign Language. Since he had no qualification to do anything else overseas, it looked as if he was in for a long session at home.

He had predicted the tears he saw in his mother's eyes as soon as she opened the front door. He smiled gently, saying she shouldn't cry. Again as he had foreseen, she was asking him what he would like to eat even before he got his cases into his bedroom.

Over a large meal, he supplemented what he had told her in his letters about his experiences in Milan, but omitting complex things. Her eyes were, as usual, rounded with interest.

The next morning, he dialled Paul's number, checking it from the last letter Paul had sent him.

"Hello?" he heard.

"Paul, this is Richard. I'm back."

"Richard." Then, "It's good to hear your voice again."

"Good to hear yours."

They arranged to meet, Paul explaining that Freda would not

be able to come because she was currently visiting her mother in the West Country.

Richard waited at a table facing the pub door, and watched the door move forward and backward several times before Paul's face appeared. Paul's eyes, behind his glasses, began to scan the room but then stopped their search. He smiled his slight smile and walked over.

They shook hands and Richard asked him what he would like. Returning to the table with the drinks, Richard raised his glass and said, "Here's to a married man!"

Paul grinned, raising his glass too. Then, "Anyway, tell me more about your experiences in Milan."

Richard obliged, but he did not refer to Margaret or the girl whose boyfriends all owned expensive cars. He then spoke about his trip to Rome.

Paul listened silently, sometimes nodding. "So," he said eventually, "another very varied experience,"

Richard looked at him and replied, "Well, yes," and, thinking about Paul's new job, said "I suppose that's what we're all trying for. I thought you'd had varied experiences too."

"I have, I guess, in a different kind of way – you know, the things I was telling you about."

Richard nodded.

"But," Paul went on, "there is a problem." His index finger went to his forehead and made an impression in the skin. "Although the situations and problems are vivid, and although they open my eyes to many things, I'm all the time aware that..." He trailed off.

"Aware of what?"

"Well, what I say may sound patronising."

"Take that risk."

"Aware, then, that the situations are ones that less intelligent people get into. Oh, I know I said I've had cases of people experiencing the same fears and anxieties that I've known, and that's all true. But I've experienced other fears and anxieties, more complex ones, and there's nothing of these in the cases I've handled. So I feel—distanced from the work, to some extent, because I can never fully identify with the clients."

"But I don't imagine you're being asked to. Just as social workers aren't."

"No. I suppose not. But I still feel uncomfortable. I always have the sense that the clients are mainly average people. Average people who've got themselves in a jam."

Paul's phrasing led Richard to recall a number of his own reflections, and he replied, "Yes, most of the people you deal with will be—inevitably—average. I think that applies to most jobs."

Paul began to nod. "So, it's a question of getting used to the fact?"

"Yes."

Paul brought his glass to his lips, swallowed some beer, and brought it away again. "Then it has to be a tacit recognition. Something you never disclose. Something your eyes must never show."

Richard nodded. "In this sense, you have to wear a mask."

"It means that one is sort of trapped, in a situation where one is forced to hide one's insights."

"You could put it that way. But," he smiled, "we're not always in that situation. Like now, for example."

Paul smiled in return. "Yes, there are breathers." He immediately added, "Look, I've probably made the picture seem worse than it really is. In fact, it's not too bad, and, as I've said, there are ways I find it pretty satisfying. It's far better than accountancy."

"You think you'll stick with it, then?"

"I think so." And, "But how about you?"

Richard paused for a moment before answering, "I don't know what I'm going to do. Job-wise, that is. I do know I want to write."

"What kind of writing?"

Richard went into some detail about the project he had set himself.

"Sounds pretty impressive," said Paul.

"If I actually complete it," with a slight smile.

"You can only have a go."

"Indeed. But if I fail, it'll be the same as not having tried. The gap that was there to start with will remain unfilled. A sobering thought."

"And," said Paul, "I suppose, from other people's standpoints too, it'll come to the same thing. If nothing is produced, society won't bother to look in your direction."

Richard nodded. Then: "If only you could know in advance whether you were going to succeed…" and trailed off, grinning. "A silly thought, I know."

"But look at it from the other side. Supposing you do produce something, and you think it's good, but other people aren't interested. Again, society won't look in your direction."

"Yes, that raises the question of who judges whether something's good."

A silence took over. Richard said nothing because he felt a number of significant ideas had been exchanged, and each required more thought. He wondered if Paul was silent for the same reason. Eventually Paul said, "Well, here you are being adventurous again." He looked down at his glass. "I wish I could be, in this kind of way."

"There's nothing, then, that you'd like to write about?"

"Nothing that I've the will-power to try," looking up.

Through Richard's mind passed images of Paul at university, and he felt that Paul was not short of things to express. What appeared to be absent, by his own admission, was the willingness to attempt expression. Richard ventured, "Might you acquire that will-power some time?"

"I might. It's just that, for now at least, I'm much more concerned about being secure—home life, job, things like that. I need the security."

CHAPTER THIRTY

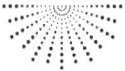

THE QUESTION OF WHAT KIND OF JOB TO SEEK WAS, FOR THE PRESENT, uppermost in Richard's mind. He appreciated Paul's point about security, though he felt he didn't need quite as much of it as Paul did: just enough for a financial basis on which to do other things.

So, what type of job? It would have to be something meaningful, even though largely a means to an end, since he would have to keep at it for quite some time: for as long as the writing project lasted. Having decided it would definitely not be E.F.L. teaching, he also ruled out other kinds of pedagogy, partly because he had no other training qualification but also because he now felt he did not want to be in classroom situations again, for the immediate future at least. Instead, he wished to turn inwards, to hold a voluntary dialogue with himself rather than an obligatory one with others. There were many things he aimed to become clear about in his own mind, and this would require silence and inner focus.

He had an idea that the majority of intelligent people, at some point in their lives, wished for a period of inwardness, to fully digest their past, fully comprehend it. This desire must be greater, he concluded, the more complex that past had been; the thicker the entanglement of different elements, the deeper the need to disentangle. As the process of extrication and clarification went on, maintaining a very public persona would be difficult, even oppressive. At the moment, he felt incapable of sustaining one; but this, he found, did not worry him.

The summer was coming to an end, and overcast skies were replacing the bright blue which, on arrival from Italy, had reminded him of the country he had just left. Now, grey clouds and chill breezes struck a more characteristically English note, one whose familiarity gave him a certain satisfaction as he huddled his shoulders slightly on walks across parks and open spaces. With a smile, he humorously considered the idea that grey skies were more conducive to inwardness than blue ones.

Out walking one afternoon, he experienced the sky-feeling again. He had not had it for a long time, and now, knowing again the pressure of overhead silence, he realised that he had almost forgotten what it was like. But, as before, he managed to contain the feeling, breathing deeply and evenly to prevent it wrenching him from equilibrium. He continued to walk forward, till the silence lost its pressure and simply persisted, weightless. This recurrent experience was, he realised, something else he would have to consider as he took stock of his past.

The question then arose: How could this area of reflection be linked with his writing project, which he must start soon? Perhaps in this way: that the search for what made the physical world tick would lead him to the reason why the history of his emotions was what it had been. What if every process had a physical basis? If so, that would apply to his emotional life. It would indicate, for example, why he had come into close relationships with Helga and Pina, Ray and Paul: why with these, rather than other kinds of people he had encountered.

His thoughts reached back to the brief reading on evolution he had done, and the notion struck him that perhaps his particular sensibility was based on a certain kind of cerebral and neurological development; that in order to understand his emotional processes, he needed to learn how his brain and nervous system worked. It followed that such comprehension was necessary to grasp, not only why he felt, but also why he thought the way he did. He had a sense that this physical understanding would not rob his thoughts and feelings of their richness: they would remain as they were even if they were seen to have a physical basis. Their possessing such a foundation would not demean them. A great deal of study would, he realised, have to be devoted to researching this idea that psychology had a physical source.

CHAPTER THIRTY-ONE

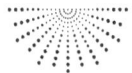

HE COMBED THE NEWSPAPERS, BOTH NATIONAL AND LOCAL, IN SEARCH of suitable work. As he read the various advertisements, he was again reminded of things he had discussed with Ray: the uncertainties that always lay ahead in one's path, the opacity of every new direction. With each ad that might be appropriate, he tried to imagine the work situation, then gave up; he had experienced enough of the unexpected to know that these efforts could only be surmises.

His eye settled on a notice for a post in local government: an administrative assistant was required in the Social Services Department of one of the London Boroughs, to work in a hostel for physically handicapped people. The job was part-time, five afternoons a week including Saturday, and consisted of a number of clerical duties. No previous experience was required, but someone with a good educational background would be preferable. It seemed the right kind of thing: not high-pressure, and secure, because it was in the public sector. But that, he reminded himself, was only how it sounded.

He wrote off for an application form, then completed and returned it. A reply letter came, inviting him for interview at the Council offices and asking him to bring proof of his qualifications.

On the day of the interview, he found himself rather nervous because, not having done this kind of work before, he was not sure what kind of questions he might be asked. But he grew calmer at the thought that at least he had been called for interview, which must indicate that he was regarded as competent for the job.

Contrary to his expectations, he was interviewed by just one person, a middle-aged man with a slight Northern accent and a mild but steady gaze. The man asked him a number of general questions, some about his social interests and attitudes, apparently taking as read the fact that he'd had no previous experience in administrative work. Richard answered in a way he thought was adequate and concise. Eventually, the interviewer smiled, stood up and extended his hand.

Three days later, he received a letter saying he had got the job. The letter also asked him to report to the hostel at 2 pm the following Monday, where the superintendent, Mr Hayes, would be expecting him.

He turned into the quiet side road in which, according to the address, the hostel was situated. He saw, about half-way along the road, a new-looking, orange brick building with lots of glass windows. A removal lorry was parked in front and some men were carrying furniture in. It seemed, then, that the hostel hadn't fully opened yet.

At the entrance, he asked one of the men, who was holding a stack of chairs, where he could find Mr Hayes, the superintendent. The man pointed to a door on the far side of the foyer. Richard walked over and knocked.

"Oh, just a minute," he heard.

Then the door opened, and a tall, slim, youngish-looking man in perhaps his mid-thirties stood smiling. He had an incipient beard. "Mr Lane?"

"Yes." And, " I was asked to report at 2pm."

"Officious-sounding word, 'report', isn't it?" Then, "Do come in." He turned with a brisk movement and walked over to where two chairs were placed beside the wall.

Richard noted the casualness of his dress: sports shirt, jeans and moccasins.

"As you see, Mr Lane, they haven't got round to putting a desk in my office. All the furniture I have at present is these chairs. Do sit down."

As Hayes sat down, Richard saw that his jeans were tight-fitting, emphasising the length of his legs.

"By the way, do call me John. May I call you Richard?"

Richard nodded, now noting that not only the first but also the second button of John's sports shirt was undone, showing a portion of his black-haired chest.

When Richard raised his eyes again to John's, the latter's were still lifting to his. He inferred that John had seen him looking at his chest; and he wondered how John had interpreted the gesture.

John crossed one leg over the other, and began turning the foot on the raised leg. At this, Richard felt he knew what John's interpretation had been. If he was right, then John had misinterpreted his gesture, and there was an error to be corrected. Thoughts of Stephens in Milan briefly passed through his mind.

"Your experience," said John, "in this kind of work is limited, I understand."

"Non-existent, actually. I'm still not sure why I was chosen."

"Intelligence and common sense," came the reply.

This told Richard that his interviewer had subsequently conferred in detail with John. "Oh, so that's what I'm assumed to have," he smiled.

John's foot went on turning slightly, but Richard made sure to confine the sight to the corner of his eye only. A misinterpretation, he realised by now, had definitely occurred.

"It's evidently what you do have," said John. He cleared his throat. "Yes, for this sort of work you don't need special expertise.

Just a grasp of everyday practicalities and—very important —the ability to get on with people."

"Well, my teaching is relevant there."

John smiled. "That's like your C.V. talking." Then, "No, but seriously, I'm sure you'll have no problems."

His eyes limpidly stayed on Richard's, but Richard did no more than nod slightly. John's forefinger went to his bristled chin, and stroked it.

There was a knock on the door. John uncrossed his legs and got up to open it. One of the men who had been carrying in the furniture told John that he and the others would be back the next day with the final batch of items. His voice was gravelly and he spoke with a heavy Cockney accent. Richard noticed that John, as he listened, seemed slightly tense in posture. When the door closed, John looked more relaxed. His eyes turned toward Richard and he put his hand on his chest, as if relieved. Then he said: "I suppose it's the way they stand there, so firmly-rooted, so four-square."

When he sat down again, his legs re-crossed, and the foot resumed turning.

Now, Richard made his eyes expressionless. John seemed about to speak again, but, looking into Richard's eyes, he hesitated.

Then he smiled, but differently from before. The foot was motionless, and he uncrossed his legs. Richard sensed the misinterpretation was over. He asked: "Could you tell me more about what the work involves?"

"By all means," replied John. He went into details. There would, he said, be some book-keeping; invoice-checking; maintaining records of rent paid by hostel residents; liaising with Head Office; completing staff time-sheets; typing letters; and various odds and ends, which, hopefully, he wouldn't mind doing.

"No, of course not," slightly amused at John's final touch of irony, and wondering if it was a mild form of retaliation for having been tacitly rebuffed. Then his thoughts moved to the people who would be coming to live in the hostel. "Will all the residents be extremely handicapped physically?"

"Some will be. Others only moderately. But all will need equal love and care."

At these last words, Richard was tempted to cast a sharp glance at John, but did not. More talk followed, covering further details about the job. During it, Richard began to wonder what John's real motivation was in holding the post of superintendent.

CHAPTER THIRTY-TWO

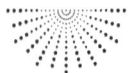

WHEN HE RETURNED THE FOLLOWING WEEK TO START WORK, RICHARD saw that a number of residents had arrived. People of various ages moved across the linoleum floors in wheelchairs. Some operated the chairs themselves; others were pushed along by care attendants. Immediately, Richard had a sense of people cut off from the social mainstream, and in a way he had not encountered before; the people he had previously known to be outside the mainstream were all able-bodied.

He walked over to John's office, and was about to knock when the door opened. John's face appeared, with a slightly flustered expression. "Oh, hello, Richard. I'll be with you in a moment, if you can hang on."

John went across to the dining room, to a table where two residents in wheelchairs were sitting. His tall figure bent down to listen to one, then to the other. He returned to Richard.

"Sorry about that. But there's some mix-up over which rooms the two residents should be in. I've been trying to sort it out." And, with a quick smile: "I think each should have the kind of room that suits his or her personality."

Richard nodded, wondering in passing how much John knew,

or thought he knew, about the personalities of the people in question.

John showed him to the room he would be working in. It was in a side-corridor, some distance from the dining room, and had a desk and chair. On the desk were a telephone and a small pile of papers which Richard assumed needed his attention.

"Well, here you are," said John. "Those papers have come over in the last few days from Head Office. The phone's for your use whenever." Again, he smiled quickly, "Can I leave you to it?"

"I think so."

"Any problems, and you know where my office is."

"Right," avoiding an ironical tone.

"By the way, you finish at six, don't you?"

"Yes."

"That's when we start serving supper. Would you like to stay for some?"

"Thanks," curious, "but I can't tonight. Perhaps another evening."

"Yes. Tell me when."

As Richard watched John leave the room, his curiosity increased. What was the reason behind John's invitation, given that he must now know that Richard was not attracted to him?

Later, on his way to the toilet, he saw, through the open door of one of the residents' rooms, John's tall figure in the middle of the carpet, head turning slightly as his eyes scanned the room. Beside him, at waist level, was the room's occupant, in a wheelchair. Richard continued on his way, not wanting John to know he had been watching him. This brief image of John made a strong impression on him – though why, he wasn't sure.

A few days later, he accepted John's invitation to stay for the evening meal and, after quite a hard afternoon's work, went into the dining room. Some residents were already at the tables, others were coming in. Richard chose an empty table in the corner near the entrance, and was served a meal by one of the care attendants.

John entered, went up to the serving hatch, and exchanged a

few joking words with the cook. Then he sat down at a table near the hatch and began talking to two of the residents already there. As he spoke, he held his head close to theirs. A meal was served to him and he picked up his fork.

Richard realised that John hadn't yet seen him. By now, the room was fairly crowded and the sound-level had risen noticeably. John, during pauses in his conversation with the two residents, started looking round the room, his eyes resting on something for a moment, then travelling on. Immediately, Richard thought of the way John's eyes had moved in the resident's room. He looked down, to avoid John catching his glance. Any second now, John would see his bent head, and would think certain thoughts.

What those thoughts would be, Richard did not know, but he was now beginning to have the idea that they might be connected with an attempt to sum people up and categorise them. He recalled what John had said about rooms fitting residents' personalities, and now thought he saw the meaning of the image of John standing in the resident's room: John's eyes were extracting as much as possible of the details of the occupant's privacy. Was a subtle prying, then, his basic motivation? And was this why he had invited Richard to stay for supper—so as to get more opportunities to observe him, more than the daily work-routine provided?

He looked up, and saw that John's eyes were on him. They turned away for a second, then returned to his, and John smiled, nodding his head, seemingly in a show of acknowledging that Richard had taken up his invitation. Richard smiled back.

Gradually, Richard got to know a number of the residents. He found, as he had elsewhere, variety in level of intelligence and in temperament. A few were highly intelligent, and with these he talked most. However, talking was difficult with some, because, as a result of their disability, they had severe speech impediments.

Some were pursuing courses of study at colleges or universities, and told him they spent long hours working in their rooms.

As he listened, Richard grew impressed by the equanimity they showed. Their solitary dedication to study reminded him of his days in the Sixth Form at school, but he appreciated that these people were separated from majority activity far more radically than he had ever been. Because of their physical condition, they had been thrown back on themselves in a much more extreme way than he had ever known; and they had come through these experiences, stayed on top of them psychologically, and now displayed even-temperedness and also humour. He wondered how he, and people such as Paul, would have fared under similar circumstances. Sometimes, while talking to them, he noticed John pass by and glance in his direction. Without returning the glance, he went on attending to what he was being told.

CHAPTER THIRTY-THREE

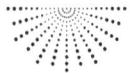

HE WAS FINDING IT DIFFICULT TO DISCIPLINE HIMSELF IN THE mornings. He wasn't organising his time sufficiently well to get enough reading done. He would, he realised, have to get up a lot earlier than he was used to, and put together a work schedule that would take account of time spent travelling to and from the library and bookshops.

Gradually, with a more systematic approach, he began to get more done, in text coverage and note-taking. He was reading books on the anatomy and physiology of the brain and nervous system; also works on the question of whether the mind was something separate from the brain or identical with it. In addition, he read further material on general evolutionary theory.

In time, a view which he had previously considered grew stronger: that the mind was not something independent of the brain, and that mental life did have a physical basis. Hence, if the latter were destroyed, mental experience would be at an end. He paused at the thought that every conscious deliverance he had ever known, every idea, sensation and emotion, had depended on a physical ticking in the brain, backed up by the operations of the nervous system. What had once seemed an incalculably complex world of its own, a free-floating kaleidoscope, now looked as if it was anchored to the brain, and perhaps enclosed completely by the latter—a brain process only.

If it was brain-dependent, then it had a far more precarious nature than he had previously thought: a single flame that could be put out, leaving only darkness. However, even if a vulnerable flame, consciousness remained something vivid, an antithesis of the blackness which surrounded it and which could engulf it at any time. Its value was enhanced by the contrast. 'Fragile but resplendent,' he murmured. And contained within it was every memory, every observation and speculation by which he could hope to make sense of the world he found himself in. As well as a flame, it was a depth and breadth of translucent layers of coloured shapes, these layers consisting of myriad upon myriad accumulations of thoughts: thoughts which continuously burgeoned from birth to death. Though constantly exposed to being shattered, like glass, it retained, while intact, its inter-imaging richness.

The question now was: what lay at the bottom of the physical processes in the brain, on which mental experience seemed to hang? This, it struck him, was the same as asking what lay at the bottom of physical processes in general, assuming they all had a common foundation. It was a question which apparently only physics could answer, and physics was a subject he knew almost nothing about. The next stage of the work, then, was to read widely in this subject. He swallowed, wondering if he would be up to the task.

The more he thought about the importance of physics, the stronger grew his impression that the brain was just one object among many in the physical world —more complex than others, perhaps, but still occupying space in the same way other objects did, and related to them in terms of basic physical constituents. However, if there was a common base-line to all physical things, what was to account for the obvious differences between people—temperament, sensibility, feeling-direction? What was to explain these clear discrepancies, the encountering of which had been such a poignant, and sometimes bitter, feature of his personal experience? Perhaps the explanation lay in the way the basic constituents were organised: different kinds of organisation being the fundamental reason for different life-paths and forms of personal affinity. Perhaps. Anyway, he would have to read on.

CHAPTER THIRTY-FOUR

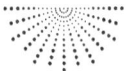

THE HOSTEL WORK WAS GOING REASONABLY WELL, BUT WAS A LITTLE tedious: it resolved into a number of procedures which were, on the one hand, clearly defined but, on the other, scarce in surprises. The weeks were passing, and soon it would be Christmas. His first thought was that he must get in touch with Paul again. Then he wondered what to buy his mother for a present.

Also, he realised that, with the end of this year, 1969, came the end of a decade. The 1960s were drawing to a close.

He regarded the 60s as the crucial decade of his life so far, mainly because of his experiences immediately before, during and after his period at university. These experiences had included his preparation for the 'A' level exams; his entry into a new and larger academic context; his first sexual encounters, both shallow and meaningful, and his first observations on the different roles that sex played in different people's lives; his first acquaintance with philosophical ideas; and his time with Pina--the most emotionally intense period of his life thus far, and one that might, for such intensity, never again be equalled. He again reflected that his relationship with her had shown how vital it was to him to have total communication with a woman, to be fully engaged in both feeling and thought; this despite the very different directions which lust often pulled him in.

The overall density of these years was something he still could not fully fathom. He still moved in the midst of it, unable as yet to stand completely outside it and circumscribe it mentally. Through the density sometimes came memories of the early and mid-1950s, and he recalled a simplicity of outlook which now he could only wonder at. He remembered the reassuring definiteness of the daily timetable in primary school; the Saturday afternoon visits to the local cinemas to see Westerns and swashbucklers; the games of cricket in the quiet road outside his house; the special creamy taste of the mashed potato that was served with school lunches. These recollections came from a world where paths had been straightforward, and the sky a friend: a world whose daily details had not shaded into ambiguity. With the gradual erosion of those certainties in the 1960s, each new day had become, not a reinforcement of the familiar, but a push into the grey area of the unknown; and, since university, a renewal of the questions which had been forged in those varsity years: Where am I basically going, and what do I amount to?

Both these questions were now bound up with his writing project. The latter offered a meaningful direction, but if it failed, he knew he would not be able to say what he amounted to. He lowered his head, trying to imagine a situation in which his final self-judgement was that he was insignificant. But, as fear at this prospect gathered, he turned his thoughts in a different direction, and felt calmer. Even so, there was the persistent sense that, whatever his ultimate self-appraisal, it was one only he could make; the path to a verdict was essentially a solitary one.

In the face of these considerations, he couldn't help but smile at many of the things that were being written and said about the 1960s in the mass media. 'The Swinging Sixties' was the most frequent phrase; 'the permissive society' a close second. These words conjured up a picture of people happily indulging themselves and achieving sexual gratification without the slightest psychological complications; a picture of easy, all-inclusive hedonism from which anxiety, self-doubt and loneliness had been magically expunged. He knew that this scenario was largely the creation of commercial interests—advertisers, and trend-setters in popular music and fashion and cinema; but it was also one which large numbers of people seemed to want to believe, perhaps because it offered an escape from complexity and sterner insights.

He recalled reading a very different view of the decade, expressed by a book publisher who had said that, with the experience of these years, optimism for the future was impossible for any thinking person. He took the publisher to be referring to, among other things, the radical increase in sexual promiscuity, an increase which he himself had both been part of and observer of, at university. This increase the publisher saw as indicating a general capacity for turpitude – an indicator which threw shadows across the future. Such a perspective, though perhaps containing an element of melodramatic overstatement, was, Richard felt, far more meaningful than the one popularly held. It implied the negative encounters which he had known, and no picture could be adequate which omitted that kind of experience. From his standpoint, shadows did indeed lie across the future. In the latter, no unqualified confidence could be placed. He had learned certain under-belly things about people, himself included, which touched the oncoming years with a sombre colouring. There would, he sensed, be no lack of future occasion for irony and scepticism.

He found himself returning to a familiar train of thought, and wondering if circumspect people of the previous generation, those who were in their early twenties in the mid and late 1940s, had thought along similar lines, as a result of observations made about many of their contemporaries. If they had, they would not now be surprised by many members of the present younger generation, who, born in the mid and late 40s, displayed the full range of perversity and weakness. A repeat performance would, it seemed, be made by the next generation. He remembered a line from the ancient Roman poet Horace, to the effect that a new batch of births is not superior to the previous one. The enormous time-distance between when this was written and now served only to reinforce the validity of the statement.

His thoughts focused again on his general age-group, and he recalled his earlier reflections, in connection with Audrey. Born during the war, she was an example of someone who had entered a world of mass slaughter and devastation, only to follow a path of superficiality. Those like himself, born a little later, had entered a world in which the global carnage had ceased, but still echoed powerfully; and many of these too had gone the superficial route. He recollected that, as a young boy in the 1950s, he had been inculcated with the idea that Allied victory in the war had been a watershed event, after which things would be better in every way than before. He had since learned that this idea was a gross oversimplification: economic conditions and job opportunities had improved, yes, but so much else--separate from the sphere of material prosperity--remained problematic. Of this the 1960s had been proof, and it looked as if the decade to come would produce no refutations.

CHAPTER THIRTY-FIVE

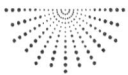

HE DROPPED PAUL A LINE ABOUT MEETING OVER CHRISTMAS. PAUL replied quickly, saying he'd very much like to but was getting ready to leave London with Freda to spend the holiday with her parents. He would get in touch in the New Year. As Richard read, he felt a tinge of something like envy for the domestic definiteness that Paul's life had gradually acquired.

He smiled slightly at the thought that he had no female apart from his mother to buy a present for. He set about thinking what to get her. Eventually, he decided on a wine-coloured scarf that he saw in a local department store. As he took the scarf over to the cashier's counter for payment, he found himself thinking of Pina, and of a necklace of brown beads he had once bought her. At the sight of the inexpensive beads, she had clasped her plump hands together, and smiled brimming with gratitude. His brow furrowed as he reflected on his decision not to write to her; but he still felt it had been the right one. He handed the scarf to the cashier, and then the money.

His mother's eyes rounded when she saw the scarf. He shouldn't have gone to all that trouble, she said. He kissed her forehead, saying it hadn't been any trouble.

He knew Christmas would be quiet, so he got some books on physics from the library to work on, at least over Boxing Day and the weekend which followed it.

During this period, and intermittently over subsequent weeks, he read about the difference between classical, Newtonian physics and the physics of modern times. He saw that one of the chief distinctions lay in the fact that classical physics had regarded the laws of nature as cast-iron and absolutely certain as a basis for calculating future events, while modern physics viewed them as providing only a probabilistic basis for prediction. It was not impossible, said modern physicists, that the regularities so far observed in nature's behaviour might cease tomorrow; however, it was highly improbable, and so, on the strength of probability, predictions could reasonably be made.

Another key feature of the modern position was its reduction of matter to energy, and its discovery that, under all known conditions, energy was conserved and never diminished or lost. Energy, then, seemed to be what all known physical processes consisted of; these would include brain processes, on which mental experience seemed dependent. What, then, was this energy? How could it be ultimately characterised? Was it perhaps like Schopenhauer's 'Will'? Further, if energy was essentially one thing, and if it was the stuff of brain processes, where lay the disparity in different people's brain processes, differences which were the source of so much non-affinity and conflict? Was the answer to be found, again, in disparities of organisation: different brains being, to a significant if not obvious extent, different structurings of energy, and therefore having different functions? If this was the case, it meant that structure determined function, and was the variable producing operational differences across the general field of energy.

Thinking about evolution, he concluded that this had been essentially the evolution of energy, the history of its permutations at the biological level. And this process had produced the mixed human picture which his own experience had presented to him.

Also, he thought again about his atheism. If everything was energy in different forms, there seemed no place for God--certainly none for any of the Gods which religions postulated; and, barring these, he failed to see what other type could possibly exist. This reinforcement of atheism confirmed his view of the surrounding natural world as a totally impersonal 'it'.

If everything was energy, then clearly its forms differed in degree of complexity: to a very considerable degree within the human sphere, but to an even greater extent between that sphere and the rest of nature. He recalled his sky-feeling, and now saw this in terms of a contrast felt by a high level of energy complexity-- himself-- in relation to a low level.

The question now arose: did energy have any pervasive purpose? Apparently not, he thought; certainly its human forms exhibited no unity of aim, nor did animal or plant life.

CHAPTER THIRTY-SIX

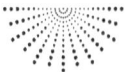

PAUL GOT IN TOUCH BY LETTER. HE BEGAN BY SAYING THAT HIS SOCIAL work office was opening a new branch in Birmingham, and he had been offered a leading post on the administrative side, which he had decided to accept. That would mean, of course, his having to leave London. He suggested a meeting. Richard, in replying to confirm that he would like to meet, reflected that Paul was now following a similar path to Ray: moving to another part of the country to work. Would that result in the ending of the relationship, as it apparently had with Ray?

When they met, Paul explained more about the job, and why he had taken it. He acknowledged that the salary was a major factor; it would enable him to save enough to buy a house. As he listened, Richard nodded, appreciating that these were good enough reasons for the decision. He felt Paul now had a clear sense of direction, even if it was, by his own admission, an emphatically safe one.

"I don't know," said Richard with a smile, "when I'll be in a position to buy a house."

"Because," Paul asked, "of the time you plan to give to writing?"

Richard nodded.

"You never know," said Paul, "your book might be a bestseller."

"But we won't bank on it."

Paul smiled. " No, but, anyhow, best of luck."

After a moment, Richard asked, "Can I have your new address?"

Paul wrote it out for him. "It's another flat we're renting. I hope it won't be too long before we can move into a house."

"When will you be leaving?"

"Next week."

As they continued talking, the question recurred to Richard: would the relationship continue? He wanted it to, even though Paul was unconnected with his main endeavours; the basic reason, he realised, was that Paul had been part of his pivotal experiences at university, and he wanted everything about those experiences to remain in the forefront of his mind.

Paul glanced at his watch. "Look. I'll have to be going. I promised Freda I wouldn't be too late back."

"Of course," finishing his drink.

They walked toward the bus stop. Richard asked Paul how he would be travelling to Birmingham.

"By car. I've put a deposit down on one, and I'm going to collect it next week."

The bus appeared in the distance. Paul held out his hand, his eyes slightly lowered, in a way which Richard recognised as indicating shyness in expressing feeling. "Again, every success with the book."

"Thanks," clasping the hand. "And I hope the new job goes okay."

Paul smiled. The bus came alongside and pulled to a halt. Paul stepped up into it, and immediately reached into his pocket for the fare. He began to turn his head back toward Richard, perhaps to wave, but the automatic doors closed quickly, cutting off Richard's view. Richard watched the bus move away.

Still wondering what the long-term course of events with Paul would be, Richard returned to his reading. Re-immersing himself in physics, he felt both intense interest and, again, loneliness: deep involvement with the subject, and at the same time a sense of being isolated by the obligation to choose and decide in ways he could not share with others. Also, he longed for the time when, having read enough in physics, he could return to a study of the arts, and so incorporate his newly acquired scientific knowledge into a perspective which also involved the humanities. The aim was an integrated, inclusive picture.

He recalled his resolve, when in Italy, to read as widely as possible in European literature, and to develop a European cultural sense. This activity would contribute to forming the overall vision. And what would this vision finally give him? Something, he hoped, which would unfailingly sustain him in the absence of belief in God.

Eventually, in his reading of physics, he came to a point beyond which it did not seem relevant to him to proceed. Having learned that matter reduced to energy, he had gone on to read that energy itself might not be the universe's ultimate and indestructible substance, even though it was self-conserving under all conditions experienced so far. If there was something to which energy reduced, the task of physics was to uncover it; yet, fascinating though this task might be, its upshot would be to show that reality had a physical basis of some kind or other, albeit not of the kind previously assumed. This general perspective was the one Richard regarded as most significant: whatever the physical foundation of things, the most interesting consideration for him was the complexity which this foundation produced at the human level, in the form of exceptional people. To study such complexity was to study outstanding human achievement across the full cultural spectrum. This examination would yield the inclusive picture he sought; it would explore the most intricate capacities the physical was known to possess, as manifested in human greatness. He must now, therefore, turn in the direction of culture—especially, though by no means exclusively, European culture; with literature occupying a special place.

CHAPTER THIRTY-SEVEN

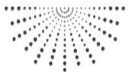

HE SPENT A NUMBER OF SUBSEQUENT WEEKS WITHOUT A SPECIFIC reading or research programme, and simply thought about the general implications of focusing on culture: its variety and history. In this area he felt more at home, sensing he could intuitively find his way about more easily than in any of the sciences. However, he continued to regard science as the crucial point of reference, and physics as the ultimate way of describing all human activity.

As his mind moved over wide areas of cultural production—books, paintings, music, sculpture—he again had the mental image which had first come to him in Italy: a mass of gems, each one catching the light in a different way. Once more, he found the image deeply satisfying. He drew pleasure from turning it over in his mind, and was not worried that, as yet, he had no explicit argument to develop. The pleasure led him to recall Schopenhauer's emphasis on contemplation as something painless, disinterested, a mental delight in the pictures and representations of reality. This delight was the stuff of culture.

He then began buying relevant books, including a recently published work by Sir Kenneth Clarke, an art historian whom he had heard praised in the media. The book was called *Civilisation* and was a survey of the major artistic achievements of Europe since the later part of the Dark Ages. Though it was relatively brief, Richard found it highly illuminating, and highly readable because of the author's informal and idiosyncratic style. Another, more specialised book he purchased was *The Civilisation of the Renaissance in Italy* by a 19th century Swiss historian named Jacob Burckhardt, who, he had previously read, had been Nietzsche's senior colleague at the University of Basle in the 1870s. This he also found engrossing.

A letter came from Paul, saying he had settled into his new job, and into his new flat. The job was satisfying: he found he enjoyed the new kind of administrative duties the work involved. Richard wrote back, referring briefly to his own work, at the hostel, but talking mainly about his new study focus on cultural history.

At the hostel, he continued to observe John's behaviour. He noted that John would ask to see individual staff members or residents in his office, and that the office door would remain shut tight, unlike the other office doors, for over half an hour at a time. Also, from written material he was asked to type up, he realised that John had extensive biographical information about residents. Again, he saw him go in and out of residents' rooms and, in the dining area, talk with residents holding his head close to theirs.

On finishing duty, John would walk upstairs to the flat he occupied on the upper floor of the hostel building. Sometimes, he would ring down to Richard on the internal line, to ask him to do certain things he had previously forgotten to mention. Over the phone, his voice would strike Richard as curiously distant, and tinged with a certain playful irony. This impression reinforced Richard's growing view that John's basic motivation was what he had first suspected it to be: a desire to pry, to penetrate people's inner lives. Behind the apparent closeness of his way of relating to people, there was a calculating detachment. Richard wondered if this had also been true of John's attempt to attract him sexually when they first met.

CHAPTER THIRTY-EIGHT

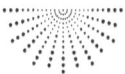

ON THE DOORMAT LAY AN ENVELOPE WITH HANDWRITING RICHARD thought he recognised. The black fountain-pen ink was vaguely familiar. He tightened in expectation and, bending to pick up the envelope, saw that it was indeed Ray's writing. Lips compressed in a smile, he quickly tore the top part and read an apology for not having communicated for so long. Ray went on to say that, while he didn't want to give excuses, it was a fact that a lot of his time had been taken up with unforeseen things: he had been posted abroad for a while, to the company's Brussels office, and he had got engaged and married. Anyway, he hoped it wasn't too late to resume their correspondence. He drew Richard's attention to his new Manchester address, in the top right hand corner of the letter.

Richard, recalling his previous view that Ray had decided to end the relationship, had no thought of not replying. The time factor didn't matter; the key point was that Ray wanted to continue where they had left off. He wrote a response the same day, saying he understood how changing circumstances could get in the way of other things, and telling him about some of his experiences in Portugal and Italy.

Within a fortnight, Ray wrote back, expressing a lot of interest in what Richard had told him, and asking questions about the political situation in Portugal. He added that he didn't know if or when he would be able to actually meet him because now, with work and family commitments, he rarely came down to London. However, he felt they could maintain ample contact by letter.

Richard concurred. He realised that, as with Paul, he would have to accept fundamental changes, and rest content with continuing the relationship in a reduced form. His reply to Ray included answers to his questions about Portuguese politics, plus information on his writing project.

He masturbated again. It was some time since he last had, because he had not felt strong desire for quite a while; but now, waking in the early hours of the morning with an erection, he felt a powerful urge. After ejaculation, he lay wondering, as he often had on similar occasions, when his sperm would flow into a receptacle other than his bed sheet.

The following weekend, the late-Spring weather was good and he decided to go to Hyde Park and sit by the Serpentine. Though not normally drawn to crowds, he had felt loneliness after a further masturbation, and now, in a general kind of way, wanted to be among people.

The sun was already quite hot when he arrived, at about 11 am. There were a lot of people sunbathing, and some swimming in the Serpentine. Several were sitting in deckchairs, but he was chary about hiring one because he knew that, over several hours, the cost would be high.

He sat down on one of the slightly-sloped areas of grass some way back from the footpath that ran along the edge of the water; then lay back, to receive the sunshine full on his face, and closed his eyes. He stretched his legs and spread his toes inside his shoes. The sound of surrounding voices trickled into his ears. He began to doze slightly, and turned over on one side. About half an hour passed.

Then, he made out what seemed a familiar voice. He opened his eyes and listened. It was a male voice with a North of England accent: a young man's. He distinguished the words: "No, you're all right, you're all right." He turned over and saw, a few yards away, a young man just under six foot tall, wearing beach shorts and vest, unfolding a blanket. He had thick eyebrows and his legs were very hairy.

'Harry,' Richard said to himself. He noted the man's nut-brown hair and heavily-jowled face. 'Harry,' he repeated silently.

Beside Harry was a girl with blonde hair and a very good figure, also wearing beach shorts. Having unfolded the blanket, Harry laid it on the grass and said, "See, there's easily enough space for two." She smiled.

Quickly, Richard thought of the period of time since he had last seen Harry, and had difficulty recalling what his situation had been when they were last in contact. Then he remembered that Harry had been about to go on holiday with Karen, the girl he had left Susan for; and that, after the holiday, had been due to attend a training course in E.F.L. at a college near Brighton.

Harry had not yet seen him, and the thought streaked through his mind that maybe he should turn over again, to avoid being recognised, and then slip away. Perhaps that would be better, to avert complications which might arise from trying to resume a relationship which had not been extremely close, and resuming it after a considerably long period of time. But before he could make a decision, Harry happened to look in his direction. His eyes fixed on his face, and his thickish lips broke into a smile.

"Richard?"

Richard smiled in return. "Harry."

"Richard!" coming over, his hand outstretched. Something in the gesture made Richard feel that Harry was at ease with the world.

They shook hands.

"Good to see you, Richard."

"Good to see you."

"What a co-incidence!" Then, "Come over and meet Marion."

Harry introduced them. Closer up, Richard was struck by Marion's facial beauty; he felt she was just as attractive as Susan or Karen, though with her own unique quality. In passing, he wondered what had happened to Harry's relationship with Karen, but knew that now was not the time to ask. At a gesture from Harry, he sat down on the blanket.

"So," said Harry, "how are things? Did you go on to do E.F.L. teaching?"

"Yes, in Portugal and Italy. Did you?"

Harry nodded. "In Turkey. Ankara." He reached over and took Marion's hand. "That's where I met this lady."

"We were teaching in the same language school," said Marion.

Richard had a sense of an experience of living and working abroad which had been entirely different from his own. He asked Harry: "How long were you there for?"

"Two years. Got the job just after I finished at the training college, and stayed there till last summer."

"I was there for just one year," said Marion. "Harry's second."

Harry went on: "I'm teaching language part-time at the moment, at a small college in central London. Marion's doing some private language tuition. And you?"

Just before answering, Richard recalled his own loss of intellectual satisfaction in E.F.L. "I'm not teaching any more. I'm doing a part-time clerical job for a Local Authority."

Harry looked a little puzzled. With a slight smile, Richard added: "Because I'm trying to do some writing."

"I knew there had to be something interesting somewhere," said Harry, now also smiling. "What kind of writing?"

"Something on philosophy, I hope." After a moment, he added, "Something that tries to connect biological evolution with culture."

Harry's eyebrows lifted slightly, and his eyes had a play of light which suggested respect for efforts he himself could not make. Richard remembered this kind of expression from the past.

"Sounds pretty deep," said Harry.

"Well, I'm trying to think long-range."

"I imagine you've read a lot of background material."

"Quite a lot, yes. But I need to read more on cultural history."

Harry nodded, eyes still with the play of light. Then, "Do you mind if I ask a question?"

"What is it?"

"Have you thought about readership? There'll probably be only a small number of takers for that kind of book."

"I know. I'm not aiming for a best-seller," reminded of a previous conversation with Paul.

Harry turned to Marion with a grin. "This is one person who's not simply going for the money," gesturing toward Richard.

She grinned too, visibly tightening her hand in his and looking only at him. At this moment, there returned to Richard a sense of Harry's genial averageness; and he had a similar sense of Marion, feeling that someone like Harry would always interest her more than even the most eminent writer could.

Harry turned back to Richard. "Anyway, the best of British with it."

At this, Richard almost smiled; the words were not, he was convinced, intended to trivialise, but were simply Harry's way of putting things.

Harry then asked, "So, what are you doing right now? Would you like a sandwich and something to drink? We've bought plenty of stuff with us," indicating a small hamper that lay at the corner of the blanket.

"Okay, thanks."

Harry brought out food packs and small bottles of beer. He passed sandwiches round, and uncapped the bottles with an opener in quick movements. When he bit into a sandwich, his jaws moved vigorously, and he looked across to Marion, asking, "Good?" She nodded, chewing more slowly. He lifted the bottle to his lips and drank deeply. Richard felt that now, in simple sensuous pleasures, Harry was completely at home.

They continued eating. Richard decided that, after finishing his food, he would not stay much longer: Harry and Marion would eventually want to be alone; also, a number of things he would like to discuss with Harry would perhaps not be of interest to her. The best thing, then, was to arrange a separate meeting with Harry.

"Another sandwich, Richard?"

"Oh, no thanks. I'm full." Then he made a gesture of looking at his watch. "Unfortunately, I'll have to be going soon." He added that he was meeting someone later in town.

"Male or female?" smiled Harry.

"Male," continuing the fabrication with a reciprocal smile. Then, "Look, we'll have to meet up."

"Sure thing."

"Where are you living?"

"In Hornsey."

"I'm not far from there."

"I know a couple of good pubs near me."

'I bet you do,' thought Richard.

Harry named a pub which Richard recalled from bus journeys through the area, and they fixed a time to meet. As he left, Marion waved in unison with Harry.

When Richard entered the pub, he saw that Harry had already arrived; he was sitting at the counter, on a stool at the far end. When Harry saw him, he raised his hand. Richard walked over.

"Hello. Been here long?" glancing at Harry's half-empty pint glass.

"No. Just thought I'd have a quick one before you came. What'll it be?"

"'Half of lager, please."

"Not a pint?"

"No, it's all right. I drink slowly."

Harry signalled to the barmaid: a short, rather plump girl

standing about half way along the bar. "A half of lager, please, and another pint of Guinness."

As the girl pulled the pumps, she glanced at Harry a couple of times; at one point, she lifted her hand to turn a lock of hair behind her ear. Harry, in turn, was looking in her direction. She served them but was immediately called to the other end of the bar. Richard was on the point of saying something about her to Harry, but then a faint smile on the latter's lips suggested there was no need: Harry had discerned her attraction to him, and regarded this kind of thing as routine. Richard decided to ask him about his time in Turkey.

"Oh, great. Fascinating country. Life's a lot simpler there – people have simple needs. They're more concerned with basic things, and do without gadgetry."

That, to some extent, reminded Richard of Portugal.

He continued, "And what were things like at the college?"

"Fine,' sipping his beer. "Just fine. I enjoyed the teaching." He laid his glass back on the counter. "And I had loads of women."

"Yeh?"

"Loads. The other teachers. There were American, British and French birds. They were just lining up – even if I say so myself."

Immediately, Richard thought of Marion, and remembered her saying she had been at the college during Harry's second year. He wondered if the women had still been lining up, as Harry put it when she was there. He decided to ask: "When exactly did Marion come?"

Harry looked at him quickly; then replied, "Actually, earlier than she was supposed to. She wasn't due until September, but she arrived during August." Then, "Are you wondering how— how she fitted in?"

Richard nodded.

"Well, I fancied her straightaway. And she did me. We started a relationship, and I cut down on the other women."

Richard noted the phrase 'cut down on'. He asked, "And Marion didn't mind continuing on that basis?"

"No." And, "She still doesn't."

"You've got other things on the go now?"

"Yes."

Richard lifted his glass and drank. He began thinking about Karen, and wondered what had happened to Harry's relationship with her.

Harry broke the silence with: "And how about you?"

"As regards women?"

"What else?"

Richard smiled slightly. "I've not been quite as busy as you. And I don't have anyone at the moment." Then, "I had a deep relationship with a girl in Portugal." He briefly talked about the relationship, and why he had decided not to continue it.

Harry listened with a look which showed genuine interest, despite the clear discrepancy between his own experience and what was being described to him. When Richard had finished speaking, he said, "Unusual, that... I suppose it's a pity, really."

Richard glanced down at his drink, in a gesture of agreement.

Silence followed. Then Harry asked: "Have you kept in touch with Paul?"

Richard replied that he had, and said that Paul was now married and living in Birmingham.

"Married, eh?"

"The girl he met at university."

"Oh, I remember." Then, "Would I be right in thinking that's been his only relationship?"

"You would be," reflecting again on the vast contrast between Paul's sexual context and Harry's. "But he's developed it to the full."

"Indeed he has."

"Another?" indicating Harry's glass.

"Yes, please."

When Richard returned with the two drinks, he ventured, "Do you mind if I ask you about your relationship with Karen?"

Again, Harry looked at him quickly. "No. You mean, what happened to it?"

"If you want to put it like that."

Harry exhaled. "It's a bit complicated. Things went wrong on our holiday."

Richard drank some of his beer, waiting for Harry to continue.

"What happened," Harry went on, "was that I slept with another girl. Someone we met at the small hotel where we were staying. She was there with her boyfriend."

"Did Karen go with anyone else?"

"No. Only me."

"Wasn't that asking for trouble?"

"Maybe, but the girl was very attractive, and she made it clear she fancied me."

"In front of her boyfriend?"

"Yes, in front of him." An expression of impatience flitted across Harry's face. "And anyway, I never want to be tied to just one person. I tried to make Karen see that. I want as wide a range of experience as I can get."

"And Karen didn't see it?"

"No," lowering his eyes.

Richard did not think he needed to ask any more questions. It seemed that Karen's insistence on an exclusive relationship had outweighed her desire. Harry quickly picked up his glass and drank a deep mouthful. Richard sensed a remembered anger in the gesture, and recalled that he had never actually seen Harry angry. But, recalling Harry's words about his subsequent experiences in Turkey, he concluded that whatever bitterness he had felt about the break-up had soon been tempered by pleasure.

Putting his glass back on the table, Harry said, "So, anyway, that was that. I really wish it could have turned out differently, but..." trailing off.

Richard thought about Harry's 'but', and realised that the word came without much difficulty to him because he could always be confident of a new girl replacing a previous one.

Harry asked, "You say you don't have anyone at the moment?"

"That's right."

"Can't be easy."

"It isn't. But I survive."

Harry nodded. "You survive. That's somewhere between witty and stoical."

"About halfway between," with a slight smile. But he wanted to change the subject, and tried to think of something new to say.

Harry spoke first: "Look, d'you fancy meeting during the day sometime. Maybe next weekend?"

"Okay. Saturday?"

"Fine."

"Where?"

"We could make it Hyde Park again, and just stroll. See the sights, as they say." He added, "The thing is, I may not be in London for much longer. I'd like to go abroad again sometime. I need adventure."

Richard sensed that this partly meant sexual adventure. Briefly, his mind returned to Harry's relationship with Marion. He replied, "Hyde Park, then. Say, the Marble Arch entrance, at noon?"

Harry nodded.

CHAPTER THIRTY-NINE

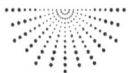

The following Saturday, the weather was again hot. Richard wore a thin pair of slacks and a short-sleeved shirt. He made his way to Hyde Park by Underground, and found the air in the carriage very stuffy.

Waiting by the Park entrance, he saw Harry approach. He was wearing beach shorts, and had on a coloured T-shirt.

"Hey-up there," smiled Harry as he came within voice-range. Richard smiled in return, remembering the expression from Harry's university days.

"Great day, isn't it?" Harry went on. "And there are already lots of birds about."

"Yes, already," wondering if Harry intended to pick someone up. If he did, was he thinking in terms of a double pick-up?

"Well," said Harry, "where shall we go first?"

"Do you want to walk along the Serpentine? We could then go on to Buckingham Palace."

"Lead the way."

As they walked, Harry's head frequently turned slightly from side to side. "It knocks me out," he said, "just how many birds there are in London. And so many of them deliciously kinky-looking." Then, "If we see a pair that look ready for it, do you want to have a go?"

Though slightly flattered at Harry's apparent assumption that he was sufficiently appealing to women to be a partner in the enterprise, Richard wondered if Harry's choice would quite coincide with his own. He did not want to be drawn into a situation where Harry felt in his element while he did not; he did not want to risk humiliation by making approaches to someone with a mind and personality totally alien to his own.

"How about it?" pursued Harry, perhaps wondering at the pause.

"Well, it depends on what we see."

After a moment, Harry replied, "There's such a thing as being too choosy."

Rather than create tension by taking issue with this, Richard decided to let the comment pass in silence. From the corner of his eye, he saw Harry glance at him, but did not turn to meet his eyes.

Was this, he wondered, the beginning of a rift? He had already noted Harry's totally uncritical response to the surrounding crowd, and he couldn't help recalling, as a contrast, his own reflections on mass-superficiality. It looked as if Harry had not trodden the hard critical terrain that he had. If this was in fact the case, it should not, Richard realised, be surprising; he had after all never associated Harry with deep mental probing.

When he turned his head again, he saw that Harry had taken off his T-shirt. His smallish brown eyes, beneath his heavy brows, had a fixed, confident look that also contained, Richard felt, a certain hardness. This was very different from the expression of sensitivity and even vulnerability they had sometimes shown. The look, Richard concluded, indicated a determination to find physical pleasure, a resolve strengthened by the many successes of the past; such successes precluded doubt or hesitation. Richard wondered what it was like to be carried along by this well-founded certainty.

They had almost walked the whole length of one side of the Serpentine, and were approaching a small, ornate bridge which led to the other side. Suddenly, Harry said, "How about those two over there? Standing on the middle of the bridge?" Richard looked in the same direction and saw two girls leaning on the bridge parapet. Both had heavy shading around the eyes. One wore long earrings which dropped almost to the nape of her neck; her hair was in a piled-up bun, with loose ringlets hanging down from her temples. The other had her hair in pig-tails, and her red-painted lips made a chewing movement.

Richard saw that Harry's eyes were fixed on both of them, seemingly sure that when they spotted him they would respond positively. Then the one with the earrings did see him, and whispered something in her friend's ear. Both looked at Harry, and the one with pig-tails stopped chewing.

Harry turned to Richard. "Do you see that?"

Richard nodded.

"So, what are we waiting for?"

Richard, conscious that they were looking only at Harry, felt that he had nothing in common with either girl, and could not share Harry's enthusiasm. He decided to say, "I haven't brought anything with me."

Harry grinned. "It's okay, I've got spares."

But still Richard did not feel he could move forward into an involvement with them, and the thought of humiliation returned. He imagined Harry's easy fluency in talking to them, and knew he could not match it.

"Which one," Harry asked, "do you fancy?"

"Neither." Then, "Look, I don't think they're interested in me anyway."

"You can change that if you want to."

"Maybe I don't want to," now feeling a nervous tension that he hoped wasn't showing.

Harry gazed at him for a moment. A slightly sardonic glimmer in Harry's eye's told him that his nervousness was obvious.

"Okay," said Harry after a moment, "not if you aren't interested. It can only work as a twosome."

Without another word, they continued walking, and crossed the bridge. As they passed the two girls, both turned their heads and looked at Harry. Richard saw that the one with long earrings wore a disappointed expression.

Richard found himself walking a little ahead of Harry as they came to the end of the bridge and began going along the other side. His sense of a rift was stronger. He did not know what to say, or what Harry might say. He recalled that he had never before had a confrontation with him, but now there could be one.

"Am I right," Harry asked, "that you're not used to casual relationships?"

Richard noted the element of tact in these words, coming as they did from someone who was overtly promiscuous.

"I haven't had that many," he replied. "But not because I haven't felt lust. I've felt that often."

"Then why?" eyes no longer with the sardonic glimmer. "If you don't mind my asking."

In response, Richard told him openly about the apprehensiveness he had felt in connection with the two girls. On finishing his description, he asked, "Does that make sense to you?"

"I think so; it sounds a bit like what I feel when I meet highly intellectual people. As if I'm going to get drawn into something I can't handle."

Richard noted that he himself did not feel nervous with the kind of people Harry described. He replied, "So, different things make us nervous."

Harry nodded.

Then, despite the tact Harry had been showing, Richard's mind returned to his lack of critical penetration; and the fact that he got on so easily with women of all kinds struck him as something inviting criticism. He said, "You seem to have an all-purpose style in your approach to women."

Harry's eyebrows rose slightly, and his eyes were subtly lit, in a way Richard recalled from the past. "I suppose I do, yes."

"And it just flows, without much effort?"

"Without much."

Richard looked at the faint smile which sat on Harry's lips before replying, "It's facile."

Harry's adam's apple moved; his eyes went opaque. Richard knew that he had never heard anything like this from him before.

"It's facile," Richard repeated, "and insipid."

Still Harry said nothing, but his eyes were not now totally opaque; a certain hardness showed in them, a hardness close to the sardonic quality they had previously had. It seemed to say: 'My success with women stands, no matter what you think'. He scratched his abdomen with the tip of his index finger. "All I know is that I've had plenty of good times, far more..." trailling off.

"Far more," offered Richard, "than I've had or will ever have?"

After a moment, "Yes."

"There's no denying that," but without bitterness; instead, he was recalling again his reflections on mass-averageness. He looked away, to focus more on these thoughts, and felt no discomfort at the ensuing silence. Walking a few yards across to a small fence, away from the crowded path, he realised the rift had definitely come and was of his own making. He did not know if Harry was still in the place he had left him. Turning, he saw he was.

He decided to go back to where Harry was standing. Coming within normal voice-range, and seeing that Harry's eyes had softened somewhat, he ventured, "You see, it's like this. The reasons our experiences have been very different are the reasons why"—he paused for a moment—"I don't think we can continue. The differences would go on showing." He paused again, looking down and then up. "They have to do with the whole way I think and feel, and with my writing. If I tried to pretend they weren't there, it just wouldn't work." He cleared his throat. "I can never be uncritical of the majority. Never."

He fell silent, waiting for a response. Harry's eyes had been on his, but with a look of being exposed and defenceless. Eventually Harry said, "Maybe you're right, that we can't continue. If we did, I think it'd be too tough-going for me."

Richard decided to reply: "I expect people to think on a wide scale. To aim at a fully worked-out philosophical viewpoint. To put the pieces together themselves. Because if they don't, they're in a grotesque situation."

"But they don't see it as grotesque. It only looks that way from your angle."

"Yes, from my angle."

"What you're asking," Harry went on, "is a lot, for most people."

"I know. But what's the alternative?"

Harry looked down. "What me and most people settle for, because we don't want to risk going out of our depth." Then, "Yes, you and I had better leave it."

"Yes, I think so."

Lifting his eyes, Harry replied, "If it meant trying that kind of thinking by myself, I just couldn't. Basically I need to be with other people, with or without big thoughts. I could never go it alone."

"Even when you saw those other people's limitations?"

"Even then. I just couldn't be critical in the way you are."

After a moment, Richard responded, "Okay."

Another silence followed. Richard turned to walk forward; then Harry did. For an instant, Richard wished he was not so intellectually exacting, but then realised that the alternative would be a betrayal of the insights he had garnered through long hours of lone meditation, meditation to which experience had inexorably driven him. There could be no going back on those insights.

They were nearing the Park gate. Richard glanced at Harry; and perceived that his eyes retained an exposed and uncertain look, which now sat, incongruously, above the torso which he had previously bared in a gesture of complete sexual self-confidence.

Richard found himself recalling another area of his past thinking: that of the risks involved in attempting unusual and original tasks. Those risks, he was certain, would never be Harry's. They came to the exit, and stopped. Richard turned to look at Harry, and saw that he was doing the same, but a shade more slowly. Richard then recollected the first moment he had seen him at university, and briefly reflected on the distancing process which now made it impossible for the feelings of that moment to be fully re-lived,

Harry asked, "What do we say now?"

"I'm not sure."

"It looks as if we're not going to see Buckingham Palace, after all."

"No," with a slight, wry smile.

"'Will you"-- he seemed to hesitate — "carry on writing?"

"Yes," not expecting the question, and wondering if Harry had asked it simply from a kind of politeness. "Yes," he echoed, "and follow wherever it takes me."

Harry nodded. Then, "Well, I'm going this way," indicating the crowded pavements of Oxford Street.

Richard nodded in his turn.

Harry placed his shirt over his shoulder. "Do you want to exchange addresses? Just in case?"

"All right," regarding this as more diplomatic than an outright 'No', and reflecting on the phrase "Just in case".

They wrote on pieces of paper and exchanged them. "Right, then," said Harry, lifting his hand in farewell without looking directly at him. He turned, and walked toward the crossing. Richard watched him reach the Oxford Street pavement, still with his shirt over his shoulder. Then his figure was lost in the crowd.

CHAPTER FORTY

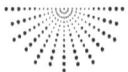

RICHARD BECAME FIRM IN HIS DECISION NOT TO WRITE TO HARRY. He did not know how he would respond if Harry wrote to him, but had a feeling he would not. On that, however, he would have to wait and see. It was clear to him that he could never again approach Harry in the same way as before, and Harry was now aware of this. Long-range critical perspective would be an inescapable factor in any future contact between them.

This factor, he realised, was present in all developed relationships among intelligent people, and was central to the way people thought about each other. It was, he also saw, fundamental to the way people thought about themselves. Quality of thought and feeling; calibre and range of achievement; degree of originality and distinctiveness: these were inevitable criteria underpinning the critical perspective.

Weeks passed, and there was no letter from Harry. Richard felt relief.

More time went by, and Richard was concerned that he had not received a letter from Paul. He reflected on the way Paul had taken on far more importance for him, psychologically, than had Harry. This was not because Paul had excelled in personal achievement but because, in sensibility, he had proved unusual, and had known unusual anxiety. Eventually, when a letter did come, it was fairly brief. It said that Freda was now pregnant. Paul also mentioned the possibility of their soon moving from a flat to a house. The letter's brevity might, Richard feared, indicate a falling-off of interest in maintaining links as Paul's domestic commitments increased.

He replied, going into some detail about the development of his writing project.

He returned to his reading – finding this now, as so often in the past, a mainstay in the midst of doubt. In addition to general books on cultural history, he began reading French fiction of the 19th century: true to his resolution to become a good European. All the time, he sought to intensify his picture of human variety and capacity, and to reach a deeper sense of what humanity could achieve. That deeper sense would—again-- be a keener apprehension of the possibilities of the physical.

In particular, as he read the works of the novelist Flaubert, he was confirmed in the distinction he had previously drawn, largely from his own experience, between exception and average. Flaubert, he saw, had an almost obsessional interest in mediocrity, in exploring its every pettiness and perversity; and Richard read him with a smile on his lips. He noted how easily Flaubert's perspective transferred to the 20th century, indeed to the small part of it which he personally knew. Also, the perspective reminded him of a number of things in the writings of Schopenhauer and Nietzsche.

Although he intended to read much more, Richard was now

developing an increasingly clear idea of the kind of book he would try to write. It would be about cultural achievements, and would place them in an evolutionary, naturalistic perspective. There would be an emphasis on the attainments of exceptional individuals, an emphasis which he knew would not be of much interest to large numbers of people.

He tried to imagine a time when the book would actually be finished: a solid entity there in front of him, the concrete result of much mental labour, groping, searching. It would be something definite to show for an enormous expenditure of thought-energy: an expenditure which, without such an upshot, would be in vain. Only when the result materialised would he feel intellectually proven; or, he felt he should say, only if it materialised.

Unsureness about the eventual outcome produced at certain moments a physical tension in his arms and stomach, and renewed his sense of the emptiness of the sky. But again he managed to accommodate the strain.

CHAPTER FORTY-ONE

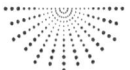

PAUL'S NEXT LETTER WAS LONGER, SOMETHING WHICH REASSURED Richard. Paul responded to various points he had made about his writing project. He also said that he and Freda had now moved into a small house, and gave quite a lot of detail about this. Reflecting on this information, plus the fact of Freda's pregnancy, Richard again had a sense of a diminished relationship with Paul: though one which, like his contact with Ray, seemed set to continue in some form or other.

Thoughts of Paul's change of address set Richard wondering about making a move himself, out of the family home and into a place of his own. Though working part-time, he was earning enough, he calculated, to afford to rent a room. Also, he was finding he needed more privacy, and was growing uncomfortable at the idea of his mother still doing everything for him domestically, even though she did it more than willingly. He wanted to regain the degree of self-sufficiency he had achieved while working abroad.

A search of advertisement cards in local shops, and of ads in the local papers, eventually bore fruit: three vacant rooms, all quite close to home, with rents well within his weekly budget, and furnished. He made phone calls, arranged to see each vacancy, and decided on one: in a small house not far from an open-air swimming pool where he used to go as a boy.

When he told his mother, she was crestfallen. She said she did not see why he shouldn't stay at home if he was continuing to live in the locality. In reply, he spoke of his wish for more self-sufficiency, and reminded her he was now in his mid-twenties. After a short silence, she asked, "Well, you will come and see me regularly, won't you?"

"Of course," gently kissing her forehead.

Packing his things together took longer than expected. He decided to leave most of his books at home, taking only those that he needed for now and the immediate future. He could always come back later to get more. He arranged transportation, and was eventually installed in his new accommodation.

He grew accustomed to having everything in one room: cooker, washbasin, wardrobe; and found this still left enough space for moving around. Also, the room was well-lit, with wide windows: something he regarded as very important. This, he meditated, would be his home for an indefinite period, and would probably be where his book, if it ever materialised, would take shape.

He became acclimatised to waking to silence and the absence of anyone else's movements; to washing and shaving, and putting the kettle on, without any voice coming his way.

At work, he continued to perform efficiently, while accepting that his duties offered no intellectual outlet. His feeling of loneliness was, he found, manageable: overlaid by a framework of routines, it was held in check and did not mar the activities required of him.

He masturbated, but less frequently than before, since he was getting fewer erections; also his orgasms were weaker, not prolonged, and with smaller ejaculations. He knew he was past the period of the very highest potency—late teens, early twenties—but not by much, and he wondered if the physical weakening was partly psychosomatic, connected with intellectual pressure, but also with a sense of isolation and a general feeling of uncertainty.

Perhaps, he reasoned, he would feel different sexually if, like a large number of people, he had a clearer sense of where he stood, socially and professionally, and of what social direction he was going in. Maybe the overall confidence that came from being strongly anchored in society would have its effect physically, relaxing him, increasing the feeling of bodily closeness to others. But he did not have that anchorage, and there was no point pretending otherwise, either to himself or to others.

He continued reading, in literature and philosophy, and more months passed, nearly a year.

His correspondence with Paul and Ray continued. Overall, Ray expressed more interest in his writing project than did Paul, a fact which confirmed his impression, formed a good while previously, of Ray's wider intellectual activity and more searching mind. In some of their letters, they almost recaptured the atmosphere of their past conversations, especially when Ray talked about the literary efforts which he had previously made and might, when he had sufficient time, resume in the future. Nevertheless, despite the more intellectual quality of his exchanges with Ray, he continued to value Paul's letters, partly because of the area of experience Paul represented.

Regularly, he visited his mother on a weekday evening, and she would prepare a meal the size of a Sunday dinner. This, he knew, indicated how much she valued his visits. On the way home one evening, he reflected that she, like himself, was basically alone, though alone at a more advanced age: her one remaining brother, who had lived nearby, had recently died, and now he was the only family she had left. He wondered how exactly she saw the years ahead – if, indeed, she contemplated the future in any detail.

Then points about her past came to mind: the jobs she had done, as a machinist, hospital domestic and, latterly, as a council home help. He also thought about the holidays she had taken him on as a child: to South coast resorts, where they had stayed in what he now remembered as rather seedy boarding houses, or in rented caravans. She was, he recalled, nearly forty when she had borne him, and it was now, when he was in his mid-twenties, that the age-gap really began to tell. This was the case even though she actually continued to look a good deal younger than she was.

With a smile, he found himself musing on other things: her taking him every week to the cinema when he was small; and her describing some of the moustached actors who appeared in these films as 'gentlemen', men who were not 'common'. Now, in retrospect, he realised that these terms denoted her largely pre-war acculturation, when cinema offered idealised heroes, often adept with a sword. Again, he thought of her age.

And, climbing the dim-lit stairs to his room, he thought also about himself. He now saw that the uncertainty which hung over his own future hung over that of older people as well.

CHAPTER FORTY-TWO

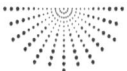

HE EVENTUALLY BEGAN MAKING NOTES FOR A FIRST DRAFT OF HIS projected work. He divided his notes into three main areas: the arts and humanities; the sciences; social and political affairs. He soon realised that the range of names and types of achievement was too wide to be captured in a single, total representation; one could only sink deep into a particular area of accomplishment, re-surface, and then sink into another. The multiplicity gave him a unique kind of excitement, as if he were being carried along by the various energies he explored, always on a new current. He had a sense that he would never lose personal momentum as long as he stayed in contact with these forces—forces that were strong but subtle, complexly potent. The linkage was crucial. It made him realise how vital it was for the individual to be able to attach himself to something greater than himself, something to drink strength from. For most people, that thing had once been religion, and for many still was; whereas for himself, and others of his outlook, the greater entity was the full corpus of human excellence.

Sensitivity to such magnitude would, it seemed, ensure a continual open-mindedness, a consistent liberality of outlook.

As his work developed, he could not help noticing other things that were happening around him: culturally, politically. There were now new fashions in pop music. The styles of the 1960s, with which he had been fully conversant as a teenager and student, had given way to different styles and new stars. At first, he found the change difficult to accept. This was not because he had ever been strongly attached to those fashions; his critical capacity had precluded that, and he had not been part of the mass adulation which the stars of the 60s had generated. It was, he realised, because those stars had become so well known, so familiar, that he had not thought it possible that anyone subsequently could arouse such interest. They had appeared to achieve the status of 'fixtures' on the social scene. But now the crowds of teenagers were turning to others, and different names were filling the music magazines and popular press; from their pages, new youthful faces beamed, with smiles affirming crowd-approval and success.

One evening at a nearby cinema, where, in the early 60s, he had seen crowds spilling over into the road and blocking the traffic in an effort to get tickets to see the latest pop sensation, he now witnessed new crowds, again bringing traffic to a standstill. He didn't bother to look up at the billboard and check who the object of adulation was this time; it was enough to note the same general phenomenon repeating itself. He reflected that what was happening now was equivalent to the displacement of 1950s stars by those of the 60s, and the eclipsing of 1940s luminaries by those of the 50s. Such, it seemed, was the way with crowds, from one generation to the next.

A few months later, something of a very different nature occupied his attention: various Middle Eastern states raised their oil prices in a gesture clearly designed to challenge the power previously exerted over them by Western governments and the major Western oil companies. The result of the price increase was inevitably a rise in fuel costs in Western countries; and he read in the papers about the Government's plans to introduce a three-day working week to make savings on industrial fuels. This, the Government said, would be a temporary measure till the economy had fully adjusted to the new prices. Within days, the shorter working week was put into operation.

As Richard thought about the defiance shown by the Middle Eastern states, he was reminded of his discussions with Helga and Pina about British imperialism in relation to, respectively, German and Portuguese imperialism. This was a subject which, he now felt, he should have given more thought to; and he began to wonder how it might relate to his project. Imperialism was clearly something to be combatted, and opposition to it was a fundamental issue. He would, he decided, do research on those people who had gone to exceptional lengths to oppose it in the past. Also, why shouldn't he himself think about being active in the same way?

His mind returned to ground it had previously covered: to the economic inequities he had experienced in Britain as well as, in a much starker form, in Portugal. These inequities were characteristic of societies with an economic hierarchy, and he knew enough about history to be aware that in both Britain and Portugal the hierarchy had been built partly on the spoils of empire, the imperialist class taking the lion's share of the wealth derived from the colonies.

He had grown up during a period when British imperial power had waned –roughly the 20 years since 1945; yet the hierarchy which that power had helped to build continued to exist, albeit in a modified form. He himself had been born into the bottom part of it, and, from an early age, had had a sense of what sort of things his family could and could not afford to buy. He could remember wondering what it would be like to be able to afford anything you wanted. Also, he recalled watching British films depicting wealthy people: people who owned large houses and employed servants, sent their children to public schools, went on spending sprees in expensive London stores, and dined in exclusive restaurants. And there had been some films, set in colonial parts of Africa, depicting Britons as the ruling group giving orders to obedient natives. He had felt distant from such people because they were nothing like the ones he met with in daily life—either at school or in the neighbourhood or at weekends, when he went with his mother to the local street market.

He recollected other things, from his teenage years: a classmate who was very good at maths but who had to give up further study and go to work because of his family's financial situation; and his own family's financial problems, highlighted by the regret he caused his mother when he withdrew from a school trip after she had paid £3 toward it and could not be re-funded the money.

As he turned these memories over, he was for a moment inclined to the view that everybody in constrained economic circumstances had an enormous amount in common simply by virtue of sharing those circumstances. The notion had a comforting, reassuring simplicity about it. But he pulled himself up, thinking of his mixed experiences at school, where the majority of people came from families in the same broad income group as his own; thinking also of the crowds of pop fans outside the local cinema—again, from roughly the same economic background as himself. So, while he clearly could not identify with the very wealthy, neither could he do so, *en masse*, with those lower down the income ladder. This, he sensed, would have been true of any society he might have been born into. Also, though he was opposed to imperialism and the economic systems it produced, he thought it unlikely that its abolition would lead to a society in which complete mutual understanding prevailed, and in which everybody attained the same cultural level. Here, he was reminded of his conversations with Pina.

CHAPTER FORTY-THREE

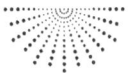

Pursuing his research into leading anti-imperialists in Britain, he went to the history and politics section of his local library. He found that the activists, ranged across a wide social and political spectrum: Marxists, socialists, liberals, and those without a specific political affiliation but taking a basic humanitarian stand. Two whose positions particularly interested him were Fenner Brockway and E. M. Forster, because of their empathetic responses to the cultures of non-European societies.

Eventually, the question returned: what could he himself do to combat imperialism? This question was inescapable, despite his feeling that the defeat of imperialism would probably not lead to a perfect society. He thought of the British colonial campaigns of the 1940s and 50s, in Malaya and Kenya—the Malayan, he noted, under a Labour government. French colonial violence in the 1950s, in Indochina and Algeria, also sprang to mind. While this violence now lay in the past, and while both Britain and France were not currently engaged in colonial war, Portugal still was, struggling to hold on to its possessions in Africa. Also, many people were saying that the United States' war in Vietnam, which had been going on since the mid-1960s, was also colonial in nature. Though not one to gain or regain formal political control of another country, as was the case with the traditional European imperialisms, it was one to secure economic control, by indirect means. And, in addition to what Western countries were doing or had done, there was also the imperialism of the Soviet Union, as evidenced in Eastern Europe after World War II, and of Communist China, as manifested in Tibet in the 1950s.

So, what to do? He recognised, with a smile, the weakness of his position: someone with only limited political knowledge, no political experience, no substantial social position or influence. He would probably have to join a political group, or groups, since he could do nothing effective by himself. And, if he did, this kind of participation might lessen his loneliness; looking around him, there seemed few other ways of reducing it, few other outlets for the extensive exchange of ideas and the intellectual commitment which were indispensable for opening the door to true companionship.

News about the Vietnam war was increasing, now again filling the newspaper headlines as it had done sporadically since the mid-60s. The fighting had reached a new level of intensity, and there was now talk of the Americans, with no prospect of victory in sight, offering to hold peace negotiations. Richard began following the headlines daily; the rumours of peace talks eventually became a reality, with Paris chosen as the venue for meetings between representatives of the U.S. and North Vietnam.

In Paris, the Americans agreed to withdraw their troops from South Vietnam – but, it seemed, not to completely end their involvement in the war. They would supply the South Vietnamese government, which many people regarded as a puppet regime, with weapons and other forms of assistance to continue the struggle against North Vietnam. The expenditure would no longer be the million dollars a day it had literally been calculated as being at the height of their war effort, when they had deployed half a million soldiers in the country. However, the outlay would still be very considerable, and a number of people were arguing that this wasn't really a withdrawal—rather, a way of maintaining indirect participation.

Richard then heard of a group called the Indo-China Solidarity Campaign, which had apparently been active on the Vietnam issue since about 1970. He got details of their meetings and decided to go along.

The meeting room was above a pub in a small road near Kings Cross Station. Although he arrived fairly early, he found that the room was almost full, with only a few chairs left at the back. He took a seat and looked around him. The people were mostly in their twenties and thirties. At the head of the room was a table with a young man, bearded, seated at one side. Richard assumed that he was the chairperson and was awaiting the arrival of the main speaker. As he looked again around the audience, he wondered which of these people he might later get into conversation with, which he might even strike up a friendship with.

A glance at his watch told him there was just a minute to go before the scheduled start of the meeting. Suddenly, people began to clap and he saw someone walking toward the speaker's table: a tallish man who was older-looking than most present, with grey, thinning hair; someone perhaps in his late forties.

The speaker was introduced as Robert Wellman. His subject, he said, would be the recent history of Vietnam and Indo-China as a whole, going back to 1939. He described how the French colonisers of Indo-China had been driven from power by the invading Japanese during World War II, and how the Japanese had themselves been ousted by Allied forces at the end of the war. He also referred to the indigenous nationalist forces in the various countries, especially Vietnam, who had fought against the Japanese occupiers during the war and, at its end, were not prepared to accept the return of the traditional colonial power, France. He then detailed how, in Vietnam, fighting subsequently resumed against the French, who were now aided by American weaponry, and how the French were decisively defeated in 1954.

He said that he himself had been a mature student at this time, and had taken part in a small campus demonstration--much frowned upon by the university authorities--in support of the nationalists.

He went on to describe how, after the French defeat, an international conference was held at Geneva, at which it was decided that elections would take place in Vietnam in 1956 for a new national Government; and how these elections failed to materialise, because of political chicanery. What followed was conflict between the nationalist forces – now predominantly Communist and with their power-base in the north of the country – and forces in alliance with the U.S., based in the south.

The conflict escalated in the early 1960s, leading U.S. President John Kennedy to send in the first contingent of explicitly American military personnel and advisers. From then on, the American military presence gradually increased, reaching its peak of half a million men under President Lyndon Johnson in the late 1960s, and including massive air power for bombing targets in both the south and the north.

Wellman argued that the entire American project in Vietnam had an economic and geopolitical basis. Vietnam and other parts of Indo-China were valued for their various natural resources, which could serve as raw materials for the U.S. economy.

On this, he quoted the words of President Dwight Eisenhower, under whose administration in the 50s America had first become involved in Vietnam. On the geopolitical side, Indo-China was considered to have enormous strategic importance as a region on the edge of Communist China--an area which the U.S. wanted to keep free of Communist influence.

In 1970, he continued, the Americans, under President Richard Nixon, widened the war by making incursions into Cambodia and Laos. Also, they intensified their bombing of North Vietnam to an unprecedented extent. But they still failed to gain the upper hand. Further, within the United States, the business community had come to regard the war effort as too costly and not worth pursuing; and public protest, at the war in general and at the loss of

American lives in particular, was growing. The result was that, by this year, 1973, the White House had come to the conclusion that it could not, for the present at least, win the war, and that it would instead try and secure what President Nixon called "peace with honour." Thus the Paris Accords had determined that the U.S. would withdraw all its troops from Vietnam, but that its client regime in the south would remain in place to continue the war, and would receive extensive help from Washington.

Wellman concluded by voicing the suspicion that the withdrawal of American forces, though officially permanent, might only be temporary; and that Washington's continuing support to the South Vietnamese government suggested that it had not given up hope of eventually defeating the nationalists. Nixon was perhaps biding his time, maybe waiting for a change in the domestic political situation, especially the attitude of the business community, as a cue for reverting to previous policies. Hence there was still a need for the Solidarity Campaign to remain active and alert. Even if Nixon did not intend to reintroduce American forces, his aid to the corrupt and brutal regime in Saigon was sufficient grounds for maintaining the Campaign's work.

Wellman sat down to general applause, but with some people clapping louder than others. Richard tried to recall how much of the Vietnam situation he could remember from his student days. He found it was very little because, at that time, he had been preoccupied with personal problems and relationships. But he did have a clear recollection of seeing, while teaching in Milan, newspaper headlines about U.S. incursions into Cambodia. The thought came to him that, if everything Wellman said was correct, here was a situation which he had neglected for too long; neglected because of that preoccupation with very private and immediate things. But then it struck him that perhaps such absorption was excusable when one was in one's late teens and early twenties; or, at least, excusable if one wasn't directly caught up in the situation.

As the applause died down, the chairperson asked for

questions from the floor, and several people spoke, mostly making cogent points and showing much more background knowledge than Richard possessed. They were, as he had already noticed, mainly older than himself, though some not that much: whatever their age, it was clear that they had found time, amid their undoubted personal concerns, to inform themselves about this issue. From their command of language as well as their knowledge, Richard got the impression that most had university degrees and were generally involved in intellectual culture.

That involvement became very clear as the question-and-answer session progressed. From the frequent use of such words as 'bourgeois,' 'contradictions,' and 'working class,' Richard could see that many were Marxists, as he remembered how often he had seen these words in the Marxist literature he had read. He could also see that there were disagreements, both amongst the Marxist contributors and between them and the speaker, on ways of interpreting certain situations and events. At moments, these disagreements became heated, to the point where what everyone had in common ––opposition to U.S. imperialism–– was obscured. Wellman, in his replies and comments, tried as best he could to emphasise the shared ground, but not everyone responded to his efforts.

The result was that the last part of his talk, which he gave after the question-and-answer session, and in which he offered suggestions about what the Campaign could do to try and alleviate the situation in South Vietnam, did not have the overall impact which, in Richard's eyes, it deserved. No action-decisions were taken on the basis of the speaker's concluding remarks, and the only practical upshot was setting a date for the next meeting.

The divisions he had seen reminded Richard of the political meeting in Portugal, and he now began to wonder if schisms were generally widespread on the Left.

People began going downstairs, in groups or singly. This dimmed his previous hope that he might get talking to a few of them. Then he cast his eyes to the end of the room, where Wellman was packing his things away. Wellman looked up, catching Richard's glance; he smiled slightly—perhaps, Richard thought, at something in his own facial expression.

Accompanied by the chairperson, Wellman came forward. "You look disappointed," he said to Richard.

Richard, slightly taken aback by this directness and candour, found himself replying, "Well, I am, a bit, but not with your talk, Mr Wellman."

"Call me Bob." And, "With what, then?"

"With the audience. The fragmented response."

"Yes," decisively. He smiled again, then glanced at the chairperson. "Would you both care for a drink?"

The chairperson nodded, and Richard did too.

Downstairs, in the bar, there were a number of people who had been at the meeting. Several nodded toward Wellman, but some, though seeing him, showed no acknowledgement, and continued their conversations.

Wellman asked Richard and the chairperson what they would like, and then went up to the bar while they got seats.

"How long," Richard asked, "has Bob been speaking on Indo-China?"

"My name's Harvey, by the way. Since the 60s. He's talked to lots of different groups."

"Here we are," said Wellman, putting down the drinks. "By the way, you are…?"

"Richard."

"Right. Anyway, Richard, what you were saying about the response—yes, it was fragmented. It often is."

Thinking about this last sentence, Richard asked, "I understand you've been talking about Indo-China for some years."

"Since the Gulf of Tonkin incident in 1964. I saw then that the Americans were planning to step up aggression. That was under Johnson, you'll recall."

In fact, Richard recollected the incident only as a newspaper headline, and only now remembered that the President had been Johnson.

Wellman continued, "It's a great problem, this disunity. A lot of the people who oppose U.S. imperialism are Marxists, like the ones tonight, but there are so many ideological divisions amongst them, and so many different groupings. They differ in their interpretations of what Marx said, and in their attitudes toward other Marxist thinkers, such as Lenin and Trotsky."

"How long has it been like this?"

"For as long as I can remember – that is, since I was a student in the 50s. At that time, you'd have expected more unity, since many people in the political Centre and on the Right were arguing that the age of ideology was over, and therefore that Marxism as a whole was outdated. So you'd have thought that, faced with this kind of intellectual attack, Marxists would have closed ranks. But they didn't."

As Richard listened to what was being said about intellectual life in the 50s, he couldn't help reflecting that, as a boy following simple daily routines at school and home, he had known nothing about any of this. He decided to ask, "Where do you stand, regarding Marxism?"

Wellman smiled slightly, and took another mouthful of beer. "A good question." He inhaled, his light-blue eyes dilating for a moment, then returning to Richard's. "In many ways, I'm sympathetic to Marx. In general, I think he's right when he says that all societies have been politically dominated by economically self-interested groups: what he calls class rule. He's also accurate in saying that the capitalist system tends toward monopoly and imperialism. Those tendencies certainly increased in the later part of the 19th century, and have come--if this is an appropriate expression- –to a full flowering in the 20th. Modern American imperialism is the latest example."

"Succeeding the old European imperialisms, such as France and Britain?"

"Exactly."

"What about Soviet imperialism?"

"Oh indeed. Of course most Marxists argue that the Soviet Union has never been a truly Marxist system, but one controlled by a self-serving elite of Party members, bureaucrats and military men. Like the majority of Marxists, I wouldn't dream of defending that set-up or the imperialism which sprang from it."

Richard paused before saying, "You said that 'in many ways' you agree with Marx. So, not in all ways."

"No. I think Marx had an oversimplified view of the working class, and of social classes in general. This simplistic position has been inherited by most of his followers. They regard the working class as being more unitary and homogenous than it really is."

Richard thought he saw what was meant, but, for the moment, said nothing.

"More homogenous," Wellman went on, "and more unified–– culturally, intellectually, morally–– than is or ever could be the case with such an enormous number of people."

A thought struck Richard, and he decided to voice it immediately: "Does that mean, then, that the groups you were referring to in your talk, the nationalists and Communists in Indo-China who have fought against the colonial powers, are not completely homogenous?"

Wellman looked at him for a moment, then again inhaled.

"I have to say, yes. There's no getting away from the fact that any large group of people is bound to be mixed. Some will be more intelligent and capable than others, some will have more moral drive, some will have wider cultural responsiveness. That, after all, was what it was like among the Allied forces in World War II, and there's no reason why things should be different in another part of the world." He paused, then gave another slight smile. "So, are you wondering what the basis is of my support for the anti-colonial forces?"

Richard nodded, seeing the other's ability to read his thoughts.

"Well, obviously one doesn't withdraw support from a group simply because they're not completely homogenous. And, mixed though they are, they're all in the broad sense anti-colonial—which is the vital thing. I'm not a Marxist or a Communist, and I accept that anti-imperialists are a varied group; but as long as they're fighting against colonialism or its puppet regimes, they have my backing. You have to take one problem at a time. The immediate one is the U.S. – Saigon regime. When that obstacle's been removed, there may well be others to follow—connected with the variable character of the victors. But the current one is what must occupy us now."

"I think I agree with you," said Richard, "but what other difficulties might occur later?"

"The sort of thing that happened, for example, in Algeria after it gained its independence from France: disagreements among the nationalists, personal rivalries, power struggles."

"Pretty big things, then."

"Yes. Any of these could happen in an independent Vietnam, and it would be foolish to rule out the possibility on an assumption that the nationalists are infallible. They certainly are not. But, to repeat, those problems don't exist at the moment, and we have to concentrate on the one that does. Also, though there may well be grave difficulties, we shouldn't automatically assume there will be. After all, if people are voluntarily fighting and risking their lives for a cause, we have to give them some credit, even if they aren't all on the same level intellectually, culturally and in other ways."

"I agree we do, but don't those differences still create complications? If people are on different levels, perhaps they have different views of what the objectives – at least long-term objectives – are. Some will have a more complex view than others, surely."

Wellman nodded. "Yes, but again, all their views have this in common- – to get rid of colonial interference, and that common ground is what we should focus on."

This time, Richard nodded too. He then offered to buy another round of drinks. The others said yes and he went to the bar. When he returned, Wellman asked him, "Look, am I right in thinking that you're primarily concerned about the differences?"

"Primarily," Richard echoed. "Because difference is what I've experienced a great deal of. In this kind of society, at any rate. Isn't it the case that society in Indo-China is in many ways simpler than ours, culturally, and that the differences that exist within it aren't as extensive as those existing here? So it's not easy to make cultural comparisons between the two."

"I think that's right. But let's bear in mind that the disparity is due partly to the much lower standard of living in Indo-China. You can't have cultural complexity in an impoverished society."

"Oh, of course, and I realise that the impoverishment is largely the result of its having suffered colonial exploitation. But, given the disparity, cultural comparison remains difficult to make. Here, we have a complex culture which draws a distinction between exception and average, between excellence and levels below it. The question is, will Vietnam and similar countries also have a culture like that, if and when they finally free themselves from imperialist dominance? Do the nationalists and the Communists want such a culture? Or do they only want what is called 'culture for the masses'?"

"All good questions," replied Wellman. "They're all, of course, bound up with the distinction which mainly liberals make between the political and the cultural: the political being the way society organises and legislates for itself, the cultural being what people do creatively, once questions of organisation and legislation have been settled, or at least partly settled"

Richard, struck by the succinctness and clarity of Wellman's expression, responded with, "You sound as if you're a liberal."

Wellman smiled more broadly than before. "I am, essentially. That's why I'm anti-imperialist, and anti-anyone imposing his will on anyone else without adequate justification."

"That would include, then, anyone imposing culturally on another?"

"Absolutely. I should add that, like any good liberal, I'm very much interested, like you, in differences, in variety."

Spurred by these words, Richard asked, "How do you see the future of liberalism?"

"I hope it'll be brighter than its recent past. Liberalism in the classic sense, as defined in the 18th and 19th centuries, has suffered some cruel blows in Europe this century: totalitarianism in Italy from 1922-45, in Germany from 1933-45, in the Soviet Union chiefly under Stalin, and in Spain since 1939."

"And Portugal," Richard added, "since I think the 1940s."

"Earlier, actually; but yes, we must include Portugal."

Richard went on, "You speak of the 20th century. But the problem goes back earlier than that, surely. You yourself referred to 19th century imperialism."

"Oh, indeed. Actually, it's significant that the major phase of Western European imperialism, from the 1880s onwards, coincided with the relative decline of liberal philosophical thought in Western Europe."

Richard smiled slightly, with increased appreciation of Wellman's knowledge.

"And we shouldn't forget," Wellman continued, "that the period since 1945 has been far from rosy. In addition to the political situation in the Soviet Union and the Iberian peninsular, U.S. imperialism took centre-stage globally, affecting not only Indo-China but also Latin America, the Caribbean, the Middle East, the Philippines. Also, bear in mind that the American and British governments, at the end of World War II, were responsible for re-instating, politically and economically, many of the people who had supported and prospered under fascism in Germany and Italy. At the same time, they dis-empowered the war-time Resistance movements in Italy and France."

Suddenly, Richard recalled his puzzlement, when living in Italy, as to why members of the Italian Resistance had not played a significant part in post-war politics. He asked, "Why were they dis-empowered, and why were pro-fascists brought back?"

"Liberals and the Left are in agreement on this one. The Resistance had been largely an independent movement, and had enjoyed wide popular support. It stood apart from the pre-war *status quo*, in which big business had been very powerful. The American and British governments wanted to re-establish that *status quo*, to tie in with big business interests in their own countries. It didn't matter to them that so many of these big-business people had been pro-fascist. The major example of this was the Krupp family in Germany. They were the leading producer of armaments under Hitler, and are once again an industrial giant. The Americans did something similar in post-war Japan."

He stopped, and smiled faintly. "Ironical, isn't it? The schoolbooks say that the war was fought to re-establish democracy and peace. The record shows it was fought largely to re-instate international big business after the disruptions caused by business's short-sighted toleration of, even flirtation with, fascism."

"Flirtation with it? Do you mean before the war?"

"Yes. U.S. investment in Germany increased by nearly 50 percent from 1929-40, which covers most of the Nazi period. British investment was also considerable. After the war, several American and British companies sued the Allied governments for having bombed their factories in Germany."

After a moment, he continued, "As a liberal, I'm just as opposed to big business as are the Left. But, unlike most of the Left, I'm not opposed to small business. As long as private enterprise is kept small, it's not a political danger, and it constitutes a kind of freedom, initiative and mobility that would otherwise not exist. It's when it gets big and internationalised that it becomes a problem. Take the present-day multi-nationals. They are politically accountable to no one, yet they are as wealthy and as powerful as many national governments. And they influence government policies. They may have lots of shareholders, as their apologists point out, but it's the wealthiest people who own most of the shares, so the structure is in no way democratic. In a nutshell, too much wealth means power over other people, which is illiberal. It's worth remembering that it was a liberal— John Dewey— and not a Marxist who said: 'politics is the shadow cast on society by big business'."

This time, Richard inhaled, looking down at his drink. He could not recall ever listening to as concentrated and as cogent a line of argument as he had just heard. If all that Wellman said was true, then one of its many implications was that the majority of people in Western society had, for nearly 30 years, been living under a skilfully contrived illusion that the millions of deaths in World War II, the stupendous destruction and dislocation, had all been compensated for by the taming of undemocratic power and the restoration or creation of free conditions in countries outside the Soviet sphere of influence.

"Care to share your thoughts?" asked Wellman.

Looking up, Richard did. As Wellman listened, his light-blue eyes had a certain grim fixity. "Yes," he responded, "yes, when one thinks about the carnage and devastation…"

He trailed off, and both fell silent. Then Harvey spoke, asking if he could get the next round of drinks. They both nodded.

Eventually, Wellman began, "There's more detail one could give, of course, but I think you've got the general picture."

"Well, give a little more. One new twist in this crime story won't make much difference."

"Okay. Take the Middle East. France and Britain had been the leading Western interests in Middle Eastern affairs up till 1945, when the Americans edged out the French and began to do the same to the British. Their success in this direction is the reason why they are now the major Western player in the politics of the region. Or take Central America: U.S. support for the Somoza family dictatorship in Nicaragua dates back to Franklin Roosevelt. Anti-democratic intervention in the Caribbean, of which Johnson's virtual invasion of the Dominican Republic in 1965 is the most recent example, goes back to Woodrow Wilson. As regards South

America, the Kennedy administration helped establish a brutal dictatorship in Brazil in the early 60s and, this year, the Nixon administration played a leading part in the assassination of Chile's democratically-elected President Allende. In the 1950s, President Eisenhower, who had been leader of the Allied forces in Europe in World War II, awarded the Legion of Merit to the dictator of Venezuela, a country rich in oil reserves. One could go on but…"

Harvey brought the drinks, and Wellman picked up his. "Look, this'll have to be my last," he said, glancing at his watch.

"Where," Richard asked, with affection and admiration in his voice, "will you be speaking next?"

"Nottingham, two days' time." And, "Am I right in thinking you're now pretty interested in the subject?"

"You are."

"Then how will you follow it up?"

"I don't know. Maybe continue attending the Solidarity Campaign meetings."

"Yes, there's that, despite the continuing divisions. You might also think of getting in touch with the more radical elements in the Labour Party. I stress 'the radical elements' because, in relation to U.S. foreign policy, the Labour leadership is hopeless, no different now from what it was when it formed the government in the 1960s and simply kow-towed to the Americans on Vietnam." Again, he looked at his watch. "Listen, here's my phone number. Give me a ring if you feel like talking more. I'm in London from time to time."

"Thank you. For everything."

Wellman and Harvey got up. Wellman added: "And if you want to read more about the post-war gangster saga of world politics, select with care from the politics and sociology sections of the major bookshops. Cheerio for now," his smile broad, as he lifted his arm before going out of the door.

CHAPTER FORTY-FOUR

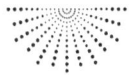

AMONG THE MANY THOUGHTS RICHARD WAS LEFT WITH WAS THE question of the psychological make-up of the nationalist forces in Vietnam. If, as Wellman said, these forces were a mixed entity, nevertheless they all showed great courage and tenacity, as Wellman also pointed out; and he found it hard to imagine most of the people he had personally encountered displaying the same. But, the thought struck him, perhaps such dedication was, among many of the Communists, due to indoctrination: an uncharitable thought, he realised, but still one that had to be considered. Perhaps many of the Communists were fighting the nationalist cause from the basis of an oversimplified view of society, of history and of the future. He recalled Wellman's reference to simplistic elements in the Marxist outlook.

He was aware that the effects of indoctrination could be immense, and could actually transform a whole society. Perhaps, he wondered with a slight smile, British society as he had known it in the 1960s could, under certain circumstances, undergo a total transformation, with people behaving in ways he never dreamed they would. However, even if this were to happen, it would not wipe out the fact that they had previously behaved otherwise, and that earlier conduct would remain an index of behavioural capacity: people only ever acted in ways they were capable of acting, and it could be safely assumed that capacity was never lost.

He brought himself up short. These were interesting thoughts, he granted, but largely speculations. He simply did not know how many, if any, Vietnamese nationalists were impelled by indoctrination; or what the effects of indoctrination might be on British society. He could be certain only about what he had experienced, and what he had garnered as indisputable fact. His mind returned to a point Wellman had insisted on: that whatever the variability among the Vietnamese nationalists, they were fighting American imperialism, a force which had to be defeated if there was ever to be any hope of freedom in that country. His own idea of freedom, probably like Wellman's, was a culturally open society from which no knowledge was barred, and one with an economic system which could support that openness by, among other things, providing equality of educational opportunity. A separate issue was that of qualitative differences in cultural performance: differences which such openness would produce. But, this issue aside, it was clear that the openness would not be possible at all if imperialism triumphed. Neither would it be possible if a rigid Left-wing ideology prevailed.

He picked up on a number of other points Wellman had made. Wellman had referred to the mixed moral quality of the Allied forces during World War II, and Richard recalled reading about the high level of venereal disease among them, especially the Americans. He had also read about certain British people who had made small fortunes selling contraceptives to troops, mainly in London. Another fact he had discovered was that the number of out-of-wedlock births had risen sharply in Britain during this period. His response to these data was not, he hoped, prudish; it was just that this kind of information added a particular shade of grey to a picture which was morally not at all black and white, and so was like the one he knew from his own experience. He reflected that, for thoughtful people during the war, such facts must have cast shadows over the future: the period in which he himself was to grow up and have, in turn, future-darkening experiences.

On what Wellman had said about business enterprise, Richard found himself agreeing that small business activity was acceptable because of the freedom and initiative it involved: drive, individuality and originality had to have an outlet, and a dreary uniformity was to be avoided. On the other hand, big business was unacceptable, because of the oppressive power-structures it generated: its freedom was other people's un-freedom.

As he considered economic activity in general, he did not forget the shadow-side of things, as he had experienced it. Even in a society where business enterprise was only small-scale, he did not imagine that relations between individuals would ever be completely free of mendacity, manipulation, illusion; and, apart from the economic sphere, he did not think that such features, including sexual infidelity, would ever be entirely absent from intimate personal relations.

His thoughts now went to the labyrinthine cunning and inexhaustible determination evinced by men bent on retaining or gaining global power. Again, if what Wellman said was true, such inexorableness had been displayed since 1945 by those who held political power in the United States, Britain, France, other Western colonial states, and in the Soviet Union. This was truly the rule of the ruthless. It called to mind the things Schopenhauer said about 'will': here was willing on a monstrous scale.

The picture now forming in his mind about the society he knew at first-hand was a sombre one: at the top level, gigantic vested interests; at lower levels, not large-scale power but widespread petty egotism. Where, then, was there genuine disinterestedness, unflagging honesty, open-mindedness and vast mental largesse? Wellman seemed to possess these qualities, but how many people were like him?

Richard regarded people of Wellman's sort as standing between those wielding enormous power and those who, though possessing little or no power, were not generous-spirited and might never be. As regards the mean-spirited in general, his mind returned to the fundamental problem of mediocrity, and he considered the possibility that society, in whatever form it took, would always have its routine-bound people, its hacks and journeymen and plodders, its rigidly unoriginal, its uninspired and uninspiring. That possibility, he reasoned, must extend as much to Third World societies, even in their post-colonial contexts, as to any others. Again, he thought of Vietnam. Even if all the nationalists were fighting with tenacity, they would still differ in general ability levels, and these differences, in a liberated Vietnam, might still produce conflict between those possessing originality and those not. Conflict might also develop between those who were mainly concerned with meeting people's basic material needs and those who placed equal or greater emphasis on fostering intellectual and cultural freedom.

Returning to the society he knew, the question was: who could replace the economically dominant groups, and create a just social order? It would have to be people of great mind, therefore people with a sense of excellence in all fields of endeavour. If such people did achieve power, what would their basic psychological relationship be with those who were small-minded and wilful-trivial? If they felt an intellectual or moral superiority toward the latter, would they show it or conceal it? And – on a different track – would they help create the kind of cultural climate to which highly intelligent but isolated individuals might relate?

These questions fell one on top of the other, each with a hefty weight. He was again, he realised, back to issues he had discussed with Pina.

The thought that he had not received another letter from her passed across his mind. She had, then, discerned his firm decision not to write. But did she still hear the intellectual echo of the conversations they had had together? This question would go unanswered.

CHAPTER FORTY-FIVE

RICHARD FOLLOWED WELLMAN'S ADVICE AND BEGAN LOOKING IN THE politics and sociology sections of the big bookshops in central London. He came across a variety of authors, mostly unfamiliar to him, and realised that here was one of many areas of thought, research and debate which he knew little about. The rows upon rows of compartments of books were at first sight daunting, and the question loomed of where to start.

In the sociology section of one of the shops, he picked up a weighty volume entitled *Treatise on General Sociology*, by an author named Pareto, who, he read in the introduction, was an Italian social and political thinker of the early part of the century. Reading on, he gathered that Pareto's main thesis was that all societies are controlled by self-interested power elites of one kind or another; and that, while particular elites change, elite-rule as such remains constant. Pareto also argued that elites rule either by predominant force or predominant guile—what he called the 'lion' or 'fox' methods. Immediately, Richard was reminded of his own sombre reflections on the social structure; but here a larger and more detailed perspective was being offered.

Pareto, it seemed, was pessimistic about elite-rule ever ending. Whereas he concurred with thinkers such as Marx that all past societies had been elite-dominated, he disagreed with Marx that such domination could ever be terminated. There would always be, he argued, certain groups who were sufficiently ruthless or cunning to claw their way to a controlling position. Also, these groups came from all social levels, and their multiplicity of origins produced a process which Pareto called 'the circulation of the elites'. Overall, Richard found these arguments intriguing and challenging.

When he had finished reading the introduction, he leafed through the pages of this very long book. Should he buy it? He felt he should. He looked at the price and realised he could just about afford it.

After paying at the cashier's desk, he drifted into the political section, running his eyes along the titles. One in particular caught his attention: *American Power and the New Mandarins*; author, Noam Chomsky. Again, he went to the introduction and, before reading very far, realised that what was being said here about contemporary U.S. imperialism was closely akin to what Bob Wellman had argued. Once more, he checked the price; it came to more than he had with him at present, but he arranged for a copy to be reserved, and he would return in a couple of days with payment.

At home, he plunged further into Pareto's *General Sociology* and saw how his overall line of argument was developed and ramified. In Pareto's presentation of a social picture in which one ruling group relentlessly replaced another, Richard was again reminded of Schopenhauerian 'will'—here depicted in the seemingly endless drive for social supremacy. Also, he saw that another way in which Pareto differed from Marx was in not regarding economic power as the only form of mastery, or control of the means of production as the only kind of dominance. As Richard recalled from his school study of history, this more complex sense of how authority could be exercised was clearly applicable to fascist regimes such as those of Hitler and Mussolini, where the economic system, though favouring big business, had been circumscribed by a political system in which big business did not have a directorial role. Pareto recognised the important degree of distinction which existed, in many regimes, between the economic and the political. Richard was additionally impressed by Pareto's prescience, with regard to people such as Hitler and Mussolini: well before the First World War, he had predicted the rise in Europe of 'lion' elites to replace the 'foxes'.

In the light of Pareto's writings, how, he wondered, could British society be characterised? He had already considered the power of vested interests and the fact of economic hierarchy. Yet there was also a parliamentary system with regular, free elections. Perhaps, however, the political process made little difference to the economic *status quo*; maybe the people who were the most influential economically had the real power in society, but subtly disguised this fact by accepting a formally democratic political system. If, then, the locus of true power was cunningly veiled, the dominant group was the 'foxes'.

He paused in this line of thought. He had used the word 'democratic', but now recalled his previous reflections on mediocrity. He felt that one could not be democratic in a totally unqualified way—that is, without acknowledging the conspicuous differences that existed in level of cultural and moral achievement. These differences had to be considered over and above a person's status as a voter and a participant in the economic system. Questions regarding moral and cultural level were crucial, and every individual, from whatever class, had finally to appear at the bar of such appraisal.

So, if he was correct in thinking that society was nowhere near as democratic as it should be, what he actually wished for was that society should be completely egalitarian in the opportunities—cultural and economic—it offered its members; but that the use of those opportunities should not lead to large concentrations of power, economic or otherwise. He remembered his agreement with Bob Wellman on the desirability of small-scale business as against large-scale, and Wellman's fundamental liberalism.

Richard again thought of Wellman when he started reading the Chomsky; he recollected Wellman's rueful comments on the position of the Allied governments in World War II, and on the war's outcome. Chomsky went into extensive detail on how American power had expanded since 1945, completely eclipsing the former world powers, Britain and France. Also, the increase in its authority had had a much greater impact on countries far beyond its borders than had that of its rival, the Soviet Union. As Richard read, he got the impression that, if Chomsky was accurate, the Allied victory had opened a veritable Pandora's box of problems: ones not as formidable as those that would have resulted from an Axis victory, but problems all the same.

There returned to him a sense of the enormity of which human beings were capable: a wilfulness that could be world-incarcerating. He thought of some lines in Shakespeare's *Hamlet*: 'Denmark's a prison.' 'Then is the world one, my lord.' And he recalled the major imperialisms of the distant past, from Egypt onward. They had been smaller-scale than modern ones only because, he realised, they had not possessed modern technology: the weaponry, plus the transportation and communication systems, which the 19th and 20th centuries had developed.

CHAPTER FORTY-SIX

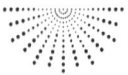

RICHARD ATTENDED ANOTHER MEETING OF THE INDO-CHINA Solidarity Campaign. This had no guest speaker, and took the form of a discussion between members. He was distressed to find that the fragmentation he had previously encountered was again in evidence, as different Marxist factions expressed disagreement with each other on a number of issues. Once more, the meeting ended inconclusively in terms of action policy.

He subsequently thought about Wellman's suggestion of making contact with radical elements in the Labour Party. There, perhaps, one wouldn't find the same degree of ideological preoccupation and conflict; for absorption in ideology seemed to be the main problem with the Solidarity people. His own thinking on social issues had brought a sense of how complex they were, and how careful one had to be when generalising. Perhaps no single ideology embraced all complexities and nuances. Maybe social reality eluded complete theoretical encapsulation, forever offering exceptions to rules, counter-examples and alternative instances. Perhaps it had inexhaustible variety, whose currents and flowings would always erode dogma. That variety, he knew from his own experience, included many situations of loneliness and pain. If, then, society was irreducibly pluralistic in character, a just body-politic would not try to deny or conceal this fact.

These manifold notions built up in Richard's mind to a point where he had to rest. They were too large and too numerous to be given exhaustive consideration in one go. He would have to return to each one separately, or maybe in small combinations, in order to think them through completely. In the meantime, he would gauge his thoughts to everyday, routine things, allowing himself to gather strength for renewed exploration.

In the weeks that followed, he deliberately kept his mind focused on his job, and on activities such as shopping, cooking, cleaning. Gradually, he came to feel an ease and relaxation which reminded him curiously of childhood. Also, he was confirmed in a previous insight: that a considerable number of people were relatively content with this same focus on the everyday—a fact which his customary involvement in intellectual projects had sometimes blurred. Many people, in shops, pubs, cafes and other places, showed by their conversation that their minds did not move extensively beyond daily facts; also, that they had little sense of exceptional levels of activity, in any field.

He re-observed this, but then let the observation drift to the margins of consciousness. He sought simple physical pleasures: jogging at the local athletics track, then showering away the sweat; drinking beer; and, normally twice a week, masturbating, now getting slightly stronger orgasms because, it seemed, of the relaxation in intellectual pressure.

He started going to football matches at his local stadium on Saturday afternoons, picking up on an activity he had periodically pursued as a boy. Standing in one of the packed terraces, he felt not only excitement at the speed and power shown by the players, but also a certain simple pleasure at the submergence of his identity in the crowd. For now, he was just one face among thousands, venting the appropriate sounds when a goal was scored or almost scored; when good and bad passes were made; when a tackle was fair or unfair. He noted that, for many of the men surrounding him, this was the highlight of their week; but he again let the perception float to the edges of his mind.

CHAPTER FORTY-SEVEN

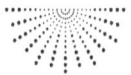

SLOWLY, HE ALLOWED HIS MIND TO RETURN TO THE SUBJECTS THAT HAD filled it. A general conclusion formed: he must campaign against big business and for a liberal culture. This would mean campaigning against imperialism. The conclusion echoed a number of things he had already pondered, but centred on what he saw as the most important of them. Factors were counterbalanced: his opposition to big business did not oblige him, on the one hand, to oppose all private enterprise or, on the other, to give uncritical support to any particular class in society. He could maintain an open attitude to all social groups, on a take-them-as-you-find-them basis. This openness applied to the past as well as the present, and was bound up with his study of exceptional achievement across the centuries. Receptiveness to the best of every age would be impossible if one had a rigidly class-bound viewpoint.

In connection with working against big business, he decided to follow up Wellman's suggestion and contact Left-wing elements in the Labour Party. Making enquiries at his local library about the nearest Party branch, he was given details about meetings. But, with this information, he was not sure whether to go along in case all those attending were Labour-mainstream and therefore not dedicated to the break-up of big business and of Western economic dominance of the Third World. Finally, he elected to take a chance.

The meeting place was above a set of offices on a busy main road which he knew well, but which he had not previously associated with political activity. It was a cold evening and he wore his overcoat. At the top of the steps, he saw the bell-sign indicating the branch office, and pressed the buzzer. A few moments later, the door opened, revealing a smallish woman of middle age.

"I've come for the branch meeting," said Richard.

"Oh, right," mildly scrutinising his face. "I don't think you've been before, have you?"

"No, first time. I've come just to listen, if that's all right."

"Yes, of course. Do come in."

He followed her through the hall and up a flight of stairs. At one point on the stairs, she turned and smiled, slightly and opaquely, then continued up. On the first floor, she led him into a large, quite well furnished room, with a set of chairs arranged around a polished brown table.

"As you see," she said, "no one else has arrived yet. By being on time, you've set a good example on your first attendance."

Richard smiled and asked, "Aren't the others usually punctual?"

"No, they're not." Then, "Would you like a cup of tea?"

"Thank you," seeing, in the corner of the room, a narrow table laid with cups and saucers, plus an electric kettle and a small sink with taps.

"By the way," she said, "my name's Edith."

"Mine's Richard."

Edith went over to the corner of the room. "Milk, sugar?"

"Both, please. One sugar."

He heard the front door open downstairs.

"That'll be another member," said Edith, "They all have keys."

The sound of footsteps on the stairs was followed by the door opening and the appearance of a tallish, well-built man with bushy grey hair. Richard put him in his forties.

"Reg," said Edith, "this is Richard. He hasn't been before."

"Reg Burrows," said the man, extending his hand.

"Pleased to meet you."

Edith gave Richard a cup of tea, then one to Burrows.

Other people started arriving—mostly, Richard noted, in their forties and fifties. Edith introduced them all to Richard, and served them tea.

Then the meeting began. Edith, acting as convenor, said that this evening's subject for discussion would be the three-day week recently introduced by the Government.

Burrows began the discussion by saying that the three-day scheme was indefensible because it meant loss of pay. "And for most ordinary working people, two days reduction is a hell of a lot."

Richard noted the phrase, "ordinary working people."

Someone else followed up Burrows's point by saying he had found that many people were experiencing boredom and even anxiety as a result of being at work for only three days instead of five. "This can lead to serious psychological problems. The Government has no right to create that sort of situation."

"And," said Burrows, "it could create a lot of bad feeling for the future. People may be a lot readier to go on strike if further wage-freezes are introduced."

Others nodded in agreement with this point. Somebody objected that the three-day week policy had been forced on the Government by financial pressures, but a reply came that, if so, the Government should cut back on defence-spending to obtain more money for buying oil to stoke the furnaces of industry.

The discussion continued for over an hour and a half, and ended with a majority decision to submit to the Party Regional Executive a resolution opposing the shorter working week and demanding that it end.

Richard noted that a few people had cast glances in his direction, perhaps because he had not contributed. He began to wonder what impression they had of him.

People were putting on their coats and preparing to leave. Not wanting to draw attention to himself, he got up and took his cup over to the corner table, where Edith was running water for washing up.

"You were very quiet," she said.

"Well, I did only come to listen."

"And," she asked, "did you like what you heard?"

"Goodnight, Edith!" people were calling from the door. "By the way, what's the subject of next month's meeting?"

"The Government's wages policy," she replied.

"Right."

"So, till then."

The door closed behind the last one to leave.

"Well, did you?" she asked again.

Curious at the persistence of her question, Richard decided to answer honestly: "To some extent, yes. But there was nothing at all about larger issues, such as the basic economic system and the relation between the Western economy and the Third World."

Edith looked at him quickly, and continued washing. "No, we hardly ever discuss things of that scope."

"Also, some people seemed rather prosaic in their outlook."

"How do you mean?"

"Reg, for example. Having a fixed concept called 'ordinary working people'. He was assuming that large numbers of people should be, and want to be, described as ordinary. It seems to me that any thinking person's horizon should be the extraordinary."

Because her head was slightly turned from him, he couldn't see the expression in her eyes, so didn't know whether or not to continue. But he decided he would. "Then there was the other chap, just noting that some people feel bored or anxious because they're spending less time at work, but apparently not considering the psychological significance of that fact."

Edith now looked at him, and smiled, but in the same unrevealing way she had on the stairs. "Would you like to wipe?" she asked.

"Okay."

"Here's a tea towel."

As she put the cups and saucers on the small draining rack, he picked them up.

"Yes," she said, "perhaps if we had a wider field of discussion, we'd attract younger members. As you see, most of us are middle-aged. For example, I'm in my fifties."

He nodded, not sure exactly how to reply to her point about people's ages.

She went on, "And about what Reg was saying, that many people want to be described as ordinary. Well, what if they don't regard the word as pejorative?"

"Then, for them, Reg's terminology is acceptable." As he spoke, he found himself recalling how, at school, people who had achieved only average marks would group together and give themselves an affirmative identity as 'non-brainy', one declaring their separateness from those who had scored high marks.

"The fact is," Edith said, "that there are lots of people who are willing to be called ordinary. And that willingness could be seen as proof of the accuracy of the description." She smiled again, but differently now: though faint, the smile seemed that of someone who had just disclosed a deep secret. "And about," she continued, "what the other man said. Yes, why is it that some people get psychological problems from spending less time at work? In cases where they don't regard their job as a real vocation—that is, something they'd be willing to do without payment—could it be that they lack sufficient inner direction, and so need to have their lives ordered for them by others?"

The smile stayed on her lips as she put the last saucer on the rack.

Richard, pondering the force of her words, replied nothing. Eventually, she asked, "Are you wondering, then, why I am in a Party that calls itself socialist?"

"I certainly am."

"Because there are still people in the Party—maybe not the ones here tonight —who are interested in the extraordinary, in talent, colour, energy, diversity. People who want to see these things have their place in the sun. That also means they believe in equality of educational and cultural opportunity. Belief in equal opportunity can be seen as a form of socialism."

Richard wondered if 'socialism' was quite the right word for what she meant.

"Do you," she asked, "emphasise this equality?"

He nodded. " But as the basis of a liberal culture."

"A liberal culture, yes. Perhaps that's what I really have in mind." Then, "To help release the energies and powers which an unfair economic system had walled in--that was why I joined the Party in 1945, the year of its landslide election victory. I was in my twenties, and full of the ideas of William Norris and the Fabians. I didn't foresee the extent to which purely economic issues would occupy the leadership's agenda, and how little they would interest themselves in cultural issues. Or how much they would pander to lowest common denominators among the electorate."

"Some people," Richard ventured, "might say you were a bit naive at the time."

She lowered her eyes. "Yes."

"Given," Richard went on, "the continuance of the same economic hierarchy. The leadership didn't alter this, and probably had no wish to. Their guiding lights weren't Morris and the Fabians, and haven't been so since."

She nodded, "Yes, the leadership. But, as I say, there are members with genuine cultural vision." She looked up. "And every time someone new comes to meetings, I wonder if it's this type of person."

Richard again remembered the way she had smiled at him on the stairs.

"I can see now," she added, "that I was right in my first impression of you. That you're mainly interested in the cultural implications of politics."

"Yes."

"Are you planning to join?"

"I don't know. The leadership remains a big problem. They're not against big business, and big business is an obstacle to the full development of a liberal culture. I've thought about making contact with the Labour Left – I've assumed they're unequivocally against big business."

"They are, but at the same time some of them don't show much interest in culture."

"Well, that's something pretty widespread."

"And you'll hear quite a lot of 'ordinary working people' phraseology among them."

"You're really dampening my hopes."

"Sorry, but these are facts, gleaned from over 30 years' experience."

Richard nodded. "Yes, what you say doesn't come as a complete surprise." Then, " Everywhere, you find people with limitations."

"Everywhere," she concurred. "It's called the human factor."

At these words, Richard looked into her pale green eyes, skin-creases raying from their corners. In her fifties, she was confirming conclusions he had already reached.

Catching his look, she smiled slightly. "It's just something you have to accept, isn't it?"

Again, he nodded.

After a moment, she asked, "How will you go about making contact with the Left?"

"I'm not sure."

"I can give you some names and phone numbers."

"Thanks." Then, "I take it you'll continue to convene these meetings?"

"Yes. I'm not strongly Left-leaning, so I stay in this position."

"But aren't you against big business?"

"I am, but…" pausing, lifting her eyes to a point past his shoulder, and just audibly sighing. "But I'm not sure how much cultural difference its abolition will make in the long run. Will it result in more Shakespeares, more Beethovens? I doubt it." Her eyes returned to his. "So, while I'm against big business, I find I can't get all that enthusiastic about the cause." Then, "Does that make sense to you?"

"It makes sense. But what about the hopes you talked about – the hopes you had in 1945?"

"I now see that they were excessive. I over-estimated the cultural energies which pre-war society had damned up. In 1945, I thought that the political changes would bring about a cultural revolution, with everyone avid for what's called high culture. Everyone, so to speak, listening to Wagner and reading Schopenhauer, as Bernard Shaw once put it. It just hasn't happened on anything like the scale I hoped it would."

Richard, while interested in the names she had mentioned, especially Schopenhauer, was tempted to answer that perhaps her disappointment was due to the fact that the economic changes since 1945 had not been very extensive. But then he recalled his own doubts about the cultural capacity of the majority, in whatever social context. So, instead he replied, "Going back to our earlier point: the abolition of big business probably won't lead to more Shakespeares and Beethovens, but it will hopefully reduce the number of social evils."

"Yes, that's another way of looking at it. Maybe my problem is that I feel too old for radical action."

"Is one ever too old?"

"Perhaps not," with another slight smile. "Anyway, let me give you those names and numbers."

CHAPTER FORTY-EIGHT

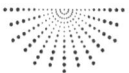

A FEW DAYS LATER, AT THE FIRST OPPORTUNITY HE HAD AFTER WORK commitments, Richard checked the list Edith had given him and randomly chose one of the names to phone: a man called George Curry. He did not quite know how to begin a phone conversation with him, and dialled the number with some apprehensiveness. After five or six rings, the receiver was picked up.

"Hello?" said a man's voice.

"Mr Curry?"

"Speaking."

"Mr Curry, I'm Richard Lane. I was given your name and number by a member of my local Labour Party branch. I'd like, if possible, to have a chat with you sometime."

"What about, exactly?"

"The outlook of the Labour Left."

"That's a pretty big subject for a chat. There's a very wide spectrum of opinion."

"Yes, I imagine there is. I know it'd be difficult to give a very detailed picture in a short space of time, but a summary of the main positions would be useful."

"Well, I can try, I suppose. Where and when?"

"Whatever's convenient for you."

"Let's see. Next Wednesday evening, there's a meeting at the Labour Club in Williams Road. That's N4. Could you make that?"

"Yes."

"D'you know where the Club is?"

"I know Williams Road. Which number?"

"285. The meeting is upstairs, and afterwards I'll be down in the bar. About 9 o'clock."

"How will I recognise you?"

"I've got a ginger beard and I'll be wearing a green sports jacket."

"Fine."

On the night, Richard caught a bus to the junction near Williams Road, then a second bus along it, knowing it was too long to walk from end to end. Through the bus window, he counted the house and shop numbers, and got off at a stop in the 260s range.

The Labour Club was set back some way from the pavement: a red-brick, two storey building with wide front windows. Through them were visible the flashing lights of a fruit machine. Entering the bar, Richard saw small groups of people at the tables along the wall. One or two people, by their unsteady way of lifting a beer glass or cigarette to their mouths, appeared to be slightly drunk. The air was quite heavy with cigarette smoke. Two youngish men stood by the fruit machine, one playing it and grinning, the other watching and chewing.

Richard ordered a half of lager. The barmaid, a woman he judged to be in her thirties, was heavily made up; she served the beer and took his money with quick, fluent gestures, then drew heavily on a cigarette which had lain perched on a nearby ashtray. He took a seat. Glancing at his watch, he noted the time was 8.50.

As he waited, he felt distinctly unimpressed by what he saw, and was reminded of similar feelings on previous occasions in pubs. The people at the fruit machine, the barmaid, the ones who were slightly drunk: these were, in broad sociological terms, 'working class', and so part of the group exploited by big business. Yet Richard found himself asking the familiar and challenging question: what exactly was their cultural level, actual or potential? Then, with Edith in mind, he wondered if the lifestyle these people would pursue in a society free of big-business domination would be much different from the one they were following now. He finished his drink.

Some people were coming down the flight of stairs at the far end of the bar. A second glance at his watch told Richard it was one minute past nine. He remembered George Curry's description of himself and kept his eyes peeled. Then, at the back of the group, he saw a green-jacketed figure, and, as the people in front parted, a ginger beard. Curry was tallish, in early middle age. He was talking to another man, who then gestured 'Goodnight' and walked along the bar to the exit. Curry's eyes followed him till he left, then went to his watch. He stood at the counter and ordered a drink.

Richard knew that Curry had no way of recognising him, since he had not given a description of himself, so it was obviously up to him to make the first move. He got up and walked over.

"Mr Curry?"

Curry turned his head.

"I'm Richard Lane"

"Oh, hello, Richard," with a quick, perhaps appraising glance. "What'll you have?"

"Half of lager, please."

Curry ordered the drink and then asked: "Do you mind if I smoke?"

"Not at all."

Curry drew a pipe and a packet of tobacco from his jacket pocket and, after filling the pipe, struck a match. "So," he said, "you'd like a sort of summary of positions held by the Labour Left."

"If that's possible."

"Possible, but not easy. Here's your lager," passing the glass to him. "No, not easy," he said again. "There's such a variety of viewpoints; socialists who are emphatically non-Marxist—some deriving their beliefs from Christian sources; socialists who partly agree with Marx; and socialists who are completely Marxist, but without wanting to leave the Labour Party and join groups like the C.P.G.B."

"Is that," asked Richard, "the Communist Party of Great Britain?"

"Yes."

"My question shows how much my knowledge needs extending."

"Actually, mine does too. I still don't know the positions of all the groups on the Far Left, and they're pretty numerous."

"But do the Labour Left groups have anything in common?"

"Yes. They'd like to see an end to all large-scale capitalism."

"Big business?"

"Big business. That of course includes the Marxists, the only difference being that they want to end all capitalism."

Reminded of Wellman's words, Richard offered to buy the next round of drinks. Curry nodded, and Richard got them from the bar.

Curry went on: "Ending big business is the objective which differentiates the Labour Left from the Labour mainstream. When the Party has been in power, the leadership has not pursued this aim. Look at MacDonald, Attlee, Wilson. Even the nationalisation programme under Attlee from '45 to '51 did no more than modestly reduce the area of control exercised over the economy by big business. Also, it created a new kind of highly paid administrative bureaucracy – people on salaries almost comparable to the top people in big business."

Richard's concentration on what Curry was saying was suddenly diminished by the sound of coins clattering down on top of one another. He turned his head and saw that the young man playing the fruit machine had just hit the jackpot, and, elated, was holding both fists out sideways.

Looking back at Curry, he said: "Sorry, you were saying."

Curry smiled, "Oh, I couldn't help noticing too. Lucky chap."

He cleared his throat. "Anyway, about that bureaucracy…"

As Curry said more about the pay-scales of the people who administered the nationalised industries, Richard couldn't help giving part of his thoughts to the jackpot winner. He had already considered the question of the youth's cultural level; and now he wondered how Curry saw him, especially in the context of his socialist views. Would the youth be welcomed into the socialist fold on equal terms with, say, other people his age who, by contrast, had distinguished themselves intellectually or morally?

"So," concluded Curry, "nationalisation didn't make that much difference to the *status quo*. Also, there's a chance that, under a future Tory government, some of the industries may be de-nationalised."

Richard paused before asking: "Well, given this entrenched economic structure, how precisely can big business be dismantled?"

Curry's lips widened from his pipe-stem into a tight smile, and his eyes narrowed slightly. "The 64-dollar question, of course. I'd like to think it can be done through parliamentary and constitutional means. But it may require violence, or some other kind of confrontation with the state. Because even if a genuinely anti-big business party were voted in, it would still face the brute economic power of the big interests, and the power of other groups whom those interests could rally to their side, such as the armed forces. You'd probably get the same reaction to, say, a general strike if it started to become effective. So the voting process and the strike might not be the way to break the economic dominance."

"The alternative, then, would mean taking on all the forces of the state, including the military."

After a moment, Curry nodded.

"Wouldn't that mean being as well armed as the military?"

"Yes."

"And well armed enough to take on the military forces of other states – for example the U.S. – who might come to the aid of the big interests here?"

"Certainly."

Richard paused to note that Curry was agreeing with him without saying more. Then he found his thoughts returning to the young man at the fruit machine, and he began to think of others who, like the youth, could not readily be associated with high exploits. He asked: "Who, exactly, would confront the state?"

"The next key question," replied Curry. "Popular forces, of course – but they would have to be very well led. Calibre of leadership would be crucial."

Richard noted with satisfaction that Curry had not answered with the blanket term 'working class'. He apparently did not have the standardised outlook which Edith had attributed to many on the Far Left. Richard then asked, "What about the calibre of the popular forces?"

"You'd need people who possessed a high level of courage, intelligence and dedication."

"That's not everyone."

"No, indeed."

Again, Richard noted the minimal way of expressing agreement.

Curry re-lit his pipe and drew on it. A silence followed, broken after about a minute by Curry's saying, "So, you see that success wouldn't be easy."

Richard nodded.

Curry went on: "In fact, I don't know if it would be possible at all."

Richard now felt he understood why Curry's replies had been so laconic. He said, "At least you're honest."

Curry again smiled tightly. "You always have to be. There's absolutely no point in feigning certainty." Then, "I suppose the thing to be getting on with now is trying to bring about the necessary changes through constitutional means. Also, something else that's needed is close co-ordination between the Labour Left groups and equivalent ones in other Western European countries. That hasn't happened yet. I'm a member of a group which is trying to get more collaboration going. It's difficult, but ultimately you've got to have international linkage. That's indispensable if your aim is not only to break big business but also to establish a genuinely co-operative world economy – which is what all socialists seek."

Richard asked him about his view of small-scale business.

"Oh, that's all right to a limited extent. There should be opportunities for small-scale competition in certain areas of the economy – mainly the production of luxury and specialist goods. There should also be space for things like small independent co-operatives and other kinds of grass-roots, local economic initiatives. But – going back to small business – because the nature of all private enterprise is to be competitive, in greater or lesser degree, it clearly couldn't be the basis for establishing worldwide collaboration. And collaboration is what's needed to avoid the over-production that comes with large-scale competition: the over-production which means rifling the planet's limited resources. Collaboration could only be achieved if the main resources were controlled by the community for the production of essential goods, with each community working in conjunction with others."

"When you say 'community', do you partly mean the people who play leading roles in it?"

"Most certainly. High-quality leadership would be as important here as in any other context. But the leadership would have to be democratically elected and continuously accountable to the electorate."

Richard found this view highly cogent, and began to think that perhaps his previous emphasis on the importance of small private enterprise had been misplaced. He asked: "Could you possibly keep me posted on your activities?"

"Of course."

Richard gave his address. Then they both finished their drinks. Curry glanced at his watch with, "And now I'm afraid I've got to be making tracks."

Richard noticed that the noise-level in the bar had increased, with more people sitting at the tables and standing at the counter, talking loudly; also, a different group was standing round the fruit machine. Shaking hands with Curry and saying goodbye, he found himself again wondering what the other thought about the youth who had hit the jackpot.

Reflecting on the overall shape of the conversation, Richard focused on what Curry had said about small business and about social leadership. He now accepted that the most important economic goal was to establish global co-operation, and that this could only be achieved by limiting competitiveness. For co-operation, collective organisation was called for. He also concurred that such organisation would require high-calibre leadership. Convinced that the majority lacked the qualities for instigating and managing momentous initiatives, he saw these qualities as residing in vanguard of exceptional individuals.

In regard to Curry's point about the democratic derivation of the leadership, the hope had to be that the majority would recognise outstanding quality when they saw it, in this field at least, and would vote accordingly. Certainly Richard could not countenance an unelected leadership--the dangers this entailed were obvious. So, elections there would have to be, but with excellence hopefully the victor.

On the cultural front, he remained uncertain of what Curry's views were, but thought that the selectivity and emphasis on quality which he had shown in his political arguments might extend to his cultural outlook. Keenness of eye in one area, which had precluded the use of stock phrases such as 'working class' and 'ordinary working people', might well mean keenness in another. So, Curry's casual comments on the jackpot winner might have been made to conceal a more stringent viewpoint which, at that moment, he had chosen not to express.

Richard's mind returned to the idea of a political vanguard, and to the recurrent question of the cultural and moral status of such a minority in relation to the majority. He now thought that the issues raised by the fact of the minority's cultural and moral superiority should be deferred, at least while the foundational aim of attaining economic collaboration and peace was being pursued. Though not fully reflecting the overall perspective of the minority, such a pursuit would be something disinterested and noble, and to this extent would voice minority values.

The question now arose of what parliamentary and constitutional means might be available for dismantling big business and achieving a mainly co-operative economy. To answer this very difficult question, he would need the help of other people, Curry included.

CHAPTER FORTY-NINE

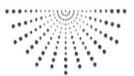

PONDERING THE QUESTION, FINDING NO OBVIOUS OR IMMEDIATE answers, he found his mind gradually returning to his book project. Recalling Edith's opinion that ending big business would not necessarily result in more Shakespeares and Beethovens, he saw the discrepancy between working on the project and trying to bring about broad economic changes. The latter task would arouse the interest of large numbers of people; the former, probably not. This was a difference he would have to accept: striving hard in two separate directions, toward separate kinds of response.

Eventually, he completed his notes for the book's first draft. He was satisfied that he had maintained a balance between the three main subject areas he had chosen, since he regarded them all as equally important. Reading through his material, he continuously heard the bass-note that was being struck: the insistence that, without exceptional individuals, society would deteriorate into a uniformity and monotony that might destroy the possibility of any further originality for generations to come. Young people with extraordinary capacities always needed precedents to awaken, guide and encourage them, and without such exemplars their abilities might lie dormant and unused.

He decided that now was the time to begin writing up. He

could make further corrections and amendments as he went along, and finally produce a finished version. It would be better, he thought, to use a typewriter than write longhand; and, checking his savings, found he had just enough to afford a small machine. He bought one at a local shop.

As he worked, he found himself frequently having to revise and re-cast: sentences, paragraphs, sets of paragraphs. This entailed learning to be very patient with himself, learning to overcome the feeling of dismay on occasions when, after a whole hour had gone by, he had found nothing pertinent to write— not a single sentence. By a slow process, he realised that to transform notes to fluent prose with tight logical coherence was not easy; while the writing sometimes flowed, it often did not.

Gradually, a fluent version began to take shape. The text's praise of the exceptional and the excellent, and its argument that the standards set by exceptional people should be the yardstick by which society measured its achievements, suddenly suggested to Richard a title for the book—something he had not previously formulated. It was simply one word: 'Aristocracy.' He was using it in its original Greek sense, meaning 'the best.' The word caught his breath; it connoted heights to which one lifted one's eyes: heights which, in his view, every society needed.

He wrote on, many ideas now falling into place which before had not been clearly ordered in his mind. He saw, with greater clarity, the link between excellence and liberalism: the latter affirmed, among other things, the right to be outstanding. This was a right to be respected not only by society as a whole but also by the body-politic.

As his work took on an increasingly definite form, he felt more of a desire to masturbate, and his ejaculations were stronger than they had been for a long time. A growth in self-confidence and hope was, he saw, the reason for this.

In the midst of his activity, he received a letter from Curry. Curry said that his group was developing links with various organisations on the Left in France and Italy. The common endeavour was to try and work out a programme of legislative proposals to curb the power of big companies in each country. When the proposals had been formulated, the intention was to campaign simultaneously for their adoption by government. Richard regarded this as a very important development. He replied to Curry, thanking him for the information, but also explaining that at present he did not have time to take part in the initiative. He added that he would still like to be kept posted, until such time as he was able to make an active contribution. Curry responded promptly, affirming that he would maintain contact by letter.

CHAPTER FIFTY

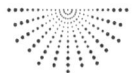

THE BOOK WAS FINISHED. IT LAY BEFORE HIM: A PILE OF TYPED SHEETS requiring, he felt, no further corrections, amendments, additions. Here at last was the fixed and definite entity he had previously envisaged.

There was now the question of finding a publisher, and Richard realised he was entering completely uncharted territory. He did not know where to look or whom to approach. He had a vague idea that he should research the market, checking which publishers were interested in which subjects, but was ignorant of how to go about this. He thought his local library might be able to give some guidance, and, when he asked, was directed to a large red volume called *The Writers and Artists Yearbook*. Here, he found lists of all U.K. publishers, plus information on the types of material they dealt with. He wasn't quite sure what category his book fitted into, and finally concluded that the best description was 'general philosophy', given that his content covered a number of different areas and integrated them into a broad picture.

He began compiling a list of all publishers who indicated philosophy as one of their specialisms, and noted which of them did not accept unsolicited manuscripts. Prioritising the latter, he wrote a series of letters giving a brief synopsis of the book.

Gradually, the replies came in, all saying more or less the same thing: the book was not suitable for their forthcoming list. He did not see how, without actually reading the text, they could be sure about its unsuitability, and had the feeling they were responding in this way because he was an unknown- –not a name that would sell. His eyes turned back to the manuscript, now bound in a folder on the table by the wall. Would it ever move on from its present location?

He decided to try the firms which had not specified 'no unsolicited manuscripts' and produced four photocopies of the text. He stopped at four, for the time being at least, because of the unexpectedly high cost of the copying. Postage was, he found, a substantial additional expense.

Within weeks, all four came back. Three had letters of the sort he was already used to. One, however, contained a longer communication saying that the subject-reader had found the book "very interesting" but unfortunately did not think it would sell enough copies to make publication viable financially. Again, Richard reflected on the fact that he was an unknown, and took this to be the implied point. But, at the same time, he was encouraged by the letter's positive content. He had, it seemed, struck a chord with at least one other person; his thought-path had been followed sympathetically by another mind, presumably a discerning one, and his way of seeing things had entered deeply into someone else's consciousness. That being the case, he had not worked in vain.

He realised with particular force how important it was for one mind to find a response in another, to receive assurance that its labours did deserve a hearing and were distinctive. He thought about the person whose efforts in an exceptional direction, no matter how prolonged, produced little effect on those of developed critical capacity; with the result that the efforts eventually ceased, silently and undemonstratively, leaving a fog of self-doubt, an absence of self-definition, a sense of life-long puerility--in the midst of which the person now had to resign himself to life's routine activities, permanently. Recalling again his conversations with Ray, he focused on the fact that this specific experience of failure applied only to those who attempted unusual things, with all the accompanying psychological risks. The experience remained unknown to those who never made such attempts: the majority.

After some time, he did three more photocopies, now having a total of seven, and tried more publishers. Again, he got one meaningful reply, a letter of the 'very interesting but...' type, and once more reflected on the implications. With a slight smile, he realised he had not foreseen how difficult it would be to get published. He looked around him, at consumer advertisements in newspapers and on street hoardings; at posters advertising films featuring sex and violence, or pulp novels or sports events. These things, he saw with a new clarity, had easy access to the public eye.

CHAPTER FIFTY-ONE

AFTER MAKING FURTHER UNSUCCESSFUL APPROACHES TO PUBLISHERS, Richard decided to drop efforts for the time being. He felt a certain fatigue, the result of building up expectations, experiencing disappointment, then repeating the process.

His mind turned back to public events. He wrote to Curry, asking him how his European efforts were progressing, and received a reply saying that the process of formulating the programme of legislative proposals to curb the power of big business was well under-way. Richard thought about offering to participate in this activity, but, for the present, did not come to a definite decision.

He was partly diverted from the subject by the news that was coming from Vietnam. The South Vietnamese regime was now clearly losing the war, being defeated in battle after battle by the North Vietnamese forces under the command of Ho Chi Minh and his leading general, Giap. The continuing U.S. support for the south was having no effect in stemming the tide.

Month after month, the Giap forces edged closer to Saigon, and it looked as if ultimate victory would soon be theirs. From many of the newspaper articles he read, Richard could see that the North Vietnamese were being characterised as evil. Remembering

Wellman's words, he knew how to respond to this characterisation. As Saigon was on the point of falling, he read that an attempt was being made to fly out hundreds of orphaned children—on the assumption, it seemed, that otherwise the 'evil' forces would butcher them once they entered the city. The next report was that a large aircraft full of children had crashed on take-off, killing all its passengers. It appeared that the crash had been due to insufficient preparation before take-off: the result of panic and fear. Richard reflected on this, the latest example of destruction and death in a war which had gone on for more than ten years.

He recalled what Wellman had said about the possibility of the U.S. directly intervening, following its 1973 military withdrawal. This did not now appear likely. If it had been going to happen, Richard reasoned, it would have by now, long before the Saigon regime began to totter. He keenly followed subsequent news stories, and saw them culminate in the reports of Giap's troops entering triumphantly into Saigon, late in 1975.

Final victory, then, had been achieved, and for the first time this century Vietnam was free of imperialist interference, either direct or indirect. In Richard's eyes, the question was now: would Vietnam, and other countries like it which succeeded in throwing off the imperialist yoke, be willing to develop a genuinely liberal culture as well as a genuinely democratic political system? He knew that, since media reports never gave a complete picture of the social situation, he would only be able to answer this question by actually going to Vietnam and seeing for himself. But this possibility was extremely remote. So, it looked as if he would have to rest content with being clear in his own mind on what he would like to see happen in that country half way across the globe.

His thoughts returned to his discussion with Curry. He considered the question of what constitutional means might be used, in Britain, to bring about basic economic change. The ideal situation was to have the right party in power, one which commanded a big majority in the House of Commons and could use this advantage to push through the requisite legislation. But which party could this be? The Labour Party's past history in power clearly made it a very doubtful candidate, unless it could be pressured into a more radical stance by its Left wing. If Labour could not be transformed in this way, it was hard to see what alternative groups were available. Even with his limited knowledge of the political scene, he was aware that none of the parties to the left of Labour had ever, on the rare occasions when they had fielded candidates at general elections, won anywhere near enough votes to stand a chance of forming a government, let alone of commanding a big majority.

A possible solution to finding a viable alternative to Labour was some kind of coalition between parties on the far Left, and the joint fielding of candidates at elections. But he could see problems here. Disagreements between parties, on ideology and other matters, might prevent the formation of such a broad front. And even if it were established, it would still have the task of winning voters away from their traditional allegiances to Labour, and of course an even more difficult one of attracting traditional Tory and Liberal voters. To achieve such an impact on the electorate would require—at least under the present voting system —far more money for campaigning and publicity than he imagined any of these groups possessed.

Also, again recalling his talk with Curry, he speculated on what might happen if this huge political transformation actually did take place. There was then the prospect of hostile action from the U.S. He knew that a number of major companies in Britain were American-owned, and he concluded that the U.S. would not sit idly by as their British branches were dismantled. Even in the case of companies which were not U.S. property, the Americans would not want to see them disappear, since they formed part of an international economic system which America wished to keep in place because of the predominant role it played in this system. Given the U.S.'s military and economic might, and its global reach—all of which had recently been evident in Vietnam—the prospect of American hostility gave pause.

CHAPTER FIFTY-TWO

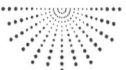

AFTER MUCH THOUGHT, HE DECIDED HE WOULD REPLY TO CURRY AND offer to take part in his work. He felt that, despite the plethora of uncertainties and unanswered questions facing him, he must be active politically. An effort must come from him in the general push to achieve, in combination, the objectives of economic co-operation and liberal culture.

At the same time, he understood the limits of politics, and knew that experience was so complex it could never be fully describable in political terms, and especially not in terms of rigid ideologies. Situations between people never reduced to simple generalisations, and could not be enclosed within tidy descriptive schemes. They would always carry surprises, good and bad, always require revision of preconceptions and re-adjustment of expectations. There would continue to be different kinds and degrees of communication between people; and, between some, hardly any at all. Such would be the case right across the social spectrum. This meant that belonging to—or being regarded as belonging to—a particular social class or group did not guarantee rapport with all other members of that group.

Also to be encountered were the lacunae of loneliness and unshared pain, the gaps in the social continuum occupied by people who, because of exceptional intelligence or problems, did not fit into everyday patterns. He recalled his own experiences of isolation, and the harrowing doubts about sexual eligibility which had afflicted Paul at university. He thought also of Pina. Further there were almost certainly several people whose paths he had crossed who were lonely, and whose loneliness he had not perceived. Even where the problems causing the isolation were eventually resolved, the encounter with them was daunting and could be protracted. It had to be gone through before a resolution came, and it would continue to be gone through.

Those who underwent this experience contrasted sharply with the people who were filled with facile self-belief and false certainties about themselves and others. Such people were conspicuously but pettily wilful, and he had little doubt that they would be as much a feature of the future as of the present.

They, like the monstrously wilful who wielded tyrannical power, had no conception of true human greatness against which to measure themselves.

Overall, society would remain a mixed picture, even if moral and intellectual excellence held political power. Perfect societies were not possible, and poor calibre of moral and cultural performance would persist, no matter how extensive economic changes were. However, this sober prospect had a positive element too: there would always be critical work to do, always failings to expose, always behaviour for the magnanimous to define themselves against. The magnanimous would make constant efforts at improvement, while knowing that perfection was out of the question; and improvement, unlike perfection, was indisputably possible.

Lifting his eyes to the future, Richard thought about other things as well. He would make further efforts to get his book published, despite the setbacks experienced so far. Here, he felt, was a work, which definitely made a difference and therefore deserved attention.

Also, now the book was behind him, he must consider moving on professionally: either to full-time work or, if he decided to have a go at another book, part-time employment of a more stimulating kind than the job he was doing now.

Then he considered his mother. He would have to think about helping her financially, and in other ways, to a greater extent than he had been called upon to do so far.

In addition to this involvement, he had the support of long-standing friendship, with Ray and Paul. He would make every effort to arrange meetings with them in the future.

However, the problem of sexual loneliness remained. His search for a meaningful relationship would be renewed, in the hope that what he had experienced separately with Pina and Helga might one day be met in combination.

THE END

AFTERWORD

This is the first book in a trilogy describing the journey of a young man into his newly discovered adult life. The boys are based on a philosophical approach to analysing how young people view the changes from adolescents to adulthood. The right and wrong discussions that effect the rest of their lives.

Book One : "INTO FULL SUNLIGHT"
    Teenage years

Book Two : "WIDE ILLUMINATION"
    University years

Book Three : "HARVESTING THE LIGHT"
    Graduation years

ABOUT THE AUTHOR TOM RUBENS

For most of my career, I have been a teacher of English, and have derived a great deal of satisfaction from this by introducing young people to the delights and mastery of British literature. In addition to working in England, I have taught in other countries. This was mainly when I was in my early 20s, and motivated by the urge that so many young people have, especially those who have just finished university, to take the plunge into completely unknown territory. I taught in Portugal and Italy; and, in the process, gained a taste for Latin Classics. Later, in my equally experimental 30s, my teaching vocation took me further afield to Nigeria, and to the very edge of the Sahara Desert. There, the huge variety of languages and cultures deepened my thirst for knowledge about the human race as a whole: including knowledge of religious and tribal ways of life . All this was very different from anything I'd experienced in Europe.

My travels helped to develop my interest in philosophy, a subject that hadn't been part of my school or university curriculum. Over many years, I have met and listened to some extraordinary and inspirational speakers on the subject. These meetings have been at lectures and events mainly held at London's Conway Hall and Royal Institute of Philosophy; and, amongst the many speakers have been Anthony Clifford Grayling CBE and Richard Dawkins Oxford's Professor for Public Understanding of Science.

In connection with their influence on me, I have always felt impelled to say things, which to my mind, absolutely needed to be articulated. This desire is bound up with my fascination for our cultural heritage in both the philosophical and literary fields.

My growing interest in philosophical sphere has chiefly been voiced in books. The first of these was published in 1984, and has since been followed by seven more publications, as well as journal articles. These broadly reflect the outlook of people such as Grayling and Dawkins: an outlook, which is based on ideas about the nature of reality.

While I worked on my philosophy synopsis texts, I also wanted to develop writing fiction. This project began solely as an effort to convey highly personal material, exploring the experiences of young people as they develop into adults. As my involvement in theorising grew, it increased my inspiration for writing a fictional account which further developed into the trilogy of novels, which includes many of the interesting subjects taught be Professor Dawkins.

My latest endeavours have been to write a trilogy of novels, based in the 1960s and 70s, about young people's experience of growing up, and their perspective in evaluating their newfound knowledge and how they interpret it. The aim of my work is to enable the reader to compare the differences between the time periods and understand better why young people make judgments and opinions today.

In philosophy, naturalism is the "idea or belief that only natural laws and forces operate in the world. In my trilogy, I hypothesis this theory associated with the re-occurring challenges, – which incidentally occur both today and 40 years ago, – in a young person's life and try to explain the processes of their thinking and the reasoning they may make.

As a final note about myself, because I think it is important to broaden my outlook on life; I volunteer for many local community activities, which focus their efforts to reduce air pollution and homelessness.

ALSO BY TOM RUBENS

Book 1 | Book 2 | Book 3

The Illumination Trilogy

The trilogy does encourage the reader to think historically about modern Western society: about the differences between the pre- and post-WW2 contexts, and especially about the periods when those differences were most marked. This stimulus is of course additional to the foci on the intricacies of personal relationships and on general philosophical ideas—which are the texts' two chief features.

These foci indicate my wish as author to show how the two things can be intimately linked, when the personal sphere has access to the public sphere of intellectually advanced culture. To repeat, that access is possible largely because the social attitudes and conditions which favour it have wide influence: as they did have in the 1960s and 70s, but as they don't have, to the same extent, in the current period.

Tom Rubens.

www.ingramcontent.com/pod-product-compliance
Lightning Source LLC
Chambersburg PA
CBHW021430080526
44588CB00009B/487